AF317049

"Having benefited from Dr. Gordon's leadership when transforming our national professional organization in the past, I know that she 'walks the walk'. After reading her book, she now 'talks the talk'! I found myself frequently nodding in agreement with her philosophy, principles, strategies and tactics for embracing true leadership qualities. This book is an enjoyable collection of poignant stories, examples, and personal insights putting the reader on the path to becoming a 'real deal' leader in whatever their chosen career may be.

—**Mark J. Lema**, MD, Ph. D., FASA, SUNY Distinguished Service Professor, Past Chair of Anesthesiology, Jacobs School of Medicine and Biomedical Sciences, University at Buffalo, SUNY, Professor of Oncology and Chair Department of Anesthesiology, Perioperative Medicine, and Pain Medicine, Roswell Park Comprehensive Cancer Center.

"Whether you are a coach, mentor, or leader, 'Being the Real Deal' provides valuable lessons for those dedicated to improving our world for all. At a time when the world needs more inspiring leaders rooted in integrity, Vicky provides a compelling and candid call for all of us to speak truth to power. Whether not-for-profit, governmental, NGOs or for-profit, the values leaders need to exhibit in their daily behaviors are exemplified in these real-life leadership stories.

—**Dorri McWhorter**, CEO, YMCA of Metropolitan Chicago, 2019 Inductee, Chicago Innovation Hall of Fame, Board Director LanzaTech, Board member, The Chicago Council on Global Affairs, featured social enterprise leader, *Uncharitable* movie.

being the REAL DEAL

THE ROOTS OF INSPIRING LEADERSHIP

being the
REAL
DEAL
THE ROOTS OF
INSPIRING LEADERSHIP
DR. VICKY GORDON

Every effort has been made to identify and attribute accurate identification of sources using APA guidelines 7th edition. The publisher apologizes for any errors or omissions and would be grateful if notified of any corrections that should be incorporated in future reprints or editions of this book. The URLs referenced in this book exist at the time of the book's initial publication but may be subject to change. Dr. Vicky Gordon, LLC does not endorse any website, blog, or link except for www.drvickygordon.com and www.vangordonmartin.com.

Library of Congress On File

Name: Gordon, Dr. Vicky, Author

Title: *Being the Real Deal: The Roots of Inspiring Leadership*

For information about this title contact the publisher:
Dr. Vicky Gordon, LLC, www.drvickygordon.com, vg@drvickygordon.com.

ISBNs:
979-8-9892059-0-5 (hardcover)
979-8-9892059-2-9 (softcover)
979-8-9892059-1-2 (eBook)

Printed in the United States of America.
Cover and Interior layout design by 1106 Design

All artwork is original (cover and book interior) by Missi Jay, Gigglebox Design
www.gigglebox.net

Dedication

For the women on whose shoulders directly I stand . . .

Vivian Estelle Perry Gordon
Nannie Lou Bunn Perry
Frances Elizabeth (Bessie) Vann Gordon
Rosa Tempie Perry
Rachel Mae Perry
Modell Gordon Parrish
Nan Gordon Hunt
Marie Beddingfield Horton
Dr. Mary Elizabeth (Pat) Jarrard
Professor Martha Nell Hardy
Dr. June Gallessich
Doris Wanda Klinkhamer
Wilma James Gordon

Contents

Prologue

Picture This . . .

You're decked out in your red power suit, briefcase in hand, as you are escorted to the Executive Director's office. You are thrilled and a little nervous about your first in-person meeting with your new coaching client. Prior phone calls with the Executive Director had identified several organizational development needs. As you walk past cubicles packed with people, you notice there is no noise—a strange silence fills the air. Your escort opens the Executive Director's office door, revealing a massive desk, a massive chair, and a small person motioning from behind the desk for you to come in and sit.

As you reach to shake hands, you cannot help but notice a six-foot portrait hanging above the credenza behind the desk. You look at the Executive Director then back at the portrait. "Yes, the portrait is of me. The staff gave it to me as a gift," explains the Executive Director with a slight smile. As you sit down, you look away, trying not to burst out laughing. Yes—this could have been a scene out of the television series The Office[1] or Seinfeld[2] but was my first in-person meeting with a new client.

Why would a leader hang this life-size portrait behind the desk? Why would staff give such a gift to their leader? The portrait story revealed itself as I interviewed staff. Adjectives used to describe the Executive Director as a leader included: narcissistic, arrogant, micromanaging, demeaning and control freak, just to list a few. But why did the staff give a life-size portrait of the Executive Director to the Executive Director?

Months earlier, the Executive Director had announced plans to leave for a CEO position. Thrilled with the news, the staff decided on a fitting departure gift—you guessed it—a life-size portrait of the narcissistic leader standing beside the massive desk in the office. An elaborate going-away celebration was held, and the gift was presented. After the event, the staff partied and joked about having gotten the last laugh.

Then the unthinkable happened. The CEO job mysteriously fell through. The Executive Director stayed and hung the portrait directly behind the desk so the staff could "see how much the gift was appreciated." The staff's joke had turned into a nightmare as they had to endure both the person and the portrait every time they were summoned to the Executive Director's office. The adage "a picture is worth a thousand words" captures the leadership lesson for the clueless Executive Director and the demoralized staff.

What portrait do your leadership behaviors paint? Do you know who you are as a leader? Do you know how others experience you as a leader? If I asked your closest colleagues to describe you as a leader, would they say, "She is the real deal" or "He is quite simply the real deal"?

What Does It Mean to Be the Real Deal as a Leader?

Being the Real Deal means you act instinctively with integrity. *Being the Real Deal* means you demonstrate your values at a profoundly deep and practical level. *Being the Real Deal* means your leadership behaviors inspire others to lead with integrity. The ability to inspire others is no longer a "nice" to have leadership compentency, but a "must" have leadership competency.

Why Is Being the Real Deal as a Leader Critical?

We Live in Dangerous Global Leadership Landscapes

We are in a moment in history where leadership standards have fallen to alarmingly low levels in public and private arenas.[3] Celebrity status is valued over public service and the common good. Lying is no longer the automatic leadership disqualifier it once was. We are losing faith in our leaders.[4]

Democracies around the world face renewed threats from totalitarian regimes and autocratic leaders. A global pandemic, climate change, threats to individual freedoms, a ground war in Europe—the list of simultaneous crises around the world seems endless.

Our Personal and Professional Lives Have Radically Changed

We have moved from a siloed, linear, assembly-line way to work and live, to an integrated supply chain, global, 24/7, interactive, and live-tweeted work, and lifestyle. Social media posts can make or break a career as well as an entire global organization's reputation. Artificial intelligence developments pose real threats.

Work and personal lives are blended and roles are blurred. Leading is now an interactive activity requiring people to be engaged, inspired and influenced—not directed and controlled.

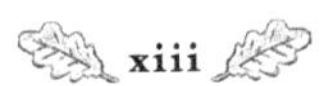

Leaders from all walks of life live in a giant fishbowl. Everything is public, even when we do our best to keep private information private. We no longer simply want to be informed; we want to be involved in meaningful ways.

Leadership development now sits at the intersection of paradoxical behaviors. As a leader, you must be collaborative and decisive; strong and humble; a listener and an advocate.

Inspiring Leadership

This book is inspired by my clients who are my treasured teachers. Sitting alone in Point Arena, California, watching the waves hit the beach, reflecting on my years of client work—this question hit me like a lightning bolt: Why do I love my clients and our work together? The answer: The leaders and the work *inspire* me. Their stories illuminate the daily leadership habits which engage others and inspire commitment. What is most needed for all leaders at all levels is a reminder to be inspired and inspire others because it is the "secret sauce" of leadership.

My career journey has many leadership settings, from the tobacco fields of North Carolina to the ivory towers of academia, to office cubicles and corporate boardrooms, to founding and leading my firm. Not many people have careers with the kind of access I have had to leaders at all levels, different types of jobs, companies, and industries. Having worked with clients from high tech to healthcare, from the shop floor to the C-suite, I have experienced a diverse group of leaders in action. By no means have I seen it all. However, my work's breadth and depth have taught me what rings true about leading, no matter who you are or what you do.

Inspiration is in short supply. Cynicism and conspiracy theories pollute people's minds. Trust in leaders is a scarce commodity. The world is in dire need of leaders who by their example call up the best in others. We must build our capacity as leaders to be inspired ourselves and inspiring to others if we are to have healthy places to work, play and live.

Leadership Roots

I grew up on a farm. Our house was surrounded by majestic oak trees planted by my grandfather. Each chapter that follows begins with an original illustration by the gifted artist Missi Jay[5] depicting aspects of an oak tree symbolic of leadership behaviors. Leading like an oak tree rooted in integrity is a powerful metaphor that can ground us as leaders.

I chose an oak tree because the oak trees on my family farm symbolize my roots—my values. Equally important is the fact oak trees throughout history and across diverse cultures are sacred. The trust we place in our leaders is sacred. Oak trees symbolize knowledge, wisdom, strength, honor, and dignity.[6] The acorn— the fruit of the oak—symbolizes growth and potential because within each acorn is all that is needed to grow into a mighty oak tree. Like the acorn, we each have the potential within us to grow as inspiring leaders rooted in integrity.

Chapter One: Leading With Mud on Your Shoes

I start our journey to becoming more inspiring as a leader by exploring the leadership example set by David Speer, CEO and Chairman of Illinois Tool Works (2006—2012). Stories are powerful teachers. David's story exemplifies what *Being the Real Deal* means. His values of integrity, humility, trust, respect, and compassion were visible and inspiring every day.

Chapter Two: Everyone Has a Story

Stories of success and values-driven leadership go beyond the accomplishments of any one CEO and allow us to see that everyone has a story. My own story begins on the farm where I was raised—where the seeds of my values were planted. No one gets to define who you are—that is your right and yours alone. "Owning your story" and "being comfortable in your own skin" is the foundation for your leadership development efforts. Your story paints a picture of your leadership roots.

Chapter Three: Either You Have It or You Don't

Integrity is the taproot of inspiring leaders. Are you honest? Do people trust you will tell "the whole truth and nothing but the truth" even if it costs you personally? *Being the Real Deal* requires leaders to cultivate an environment where honesty is the only policy—where all are expected to speak truth to power. Trust is an outcome built by being consistently honest and transparent about your purpose—your why.

Chapter Four: The Heart of the Matter

As leaders, we are inspired by the heart of the matter—a passionate purpose. Generating passion and commitment in others takes more than charisma or fiery rhetoric. Loving the work, feeling valued, and knowing what you do makes a difference are keys to inspiring others. Courage is needed every day to live our values and achieve our why.

Chapter Five: Paying the Price

Courage fuels the way forward. Until the Covid-19 pandemic made real-time heroes[7] of everyday folks, everyday courage was underappreciated. The bus driver, the grocery clerk, the ICU nurse, the sanitation worker, and the elementary school teacher just to name a few jobs that require courage to show up for work during a global pandemic. Doing your job while facing the threat of a deadly virus is courageous. Sometimes showing up takes all the courage one can muster. *Being the Real Deal* requires the courage to show up, speak up and lead with integrity.

Chapter Six: Ending and Beginnings

Conventional wisdom emphasizes the beginning of a leader's tenure as one of the most important determinants of a leader's success. How you *leave* a leadership role can be an even bigger opportunity for transformational change than the beginning. Rejecting the "lame-duck" status means checking your ego at the door and choosing to create a legacy of integrity, humility, and added value. Leading every day—even on your last day in your leadership role—grounds you in humility.

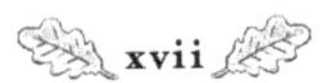

Chapter Seven: Chronic Student

We are all capable of learning every day. Saying "I don't know" sparks inspiring inquiries. Humility is required to be a "chronic student." Having coached a wide range of individuals considered to be high-potential leaders, the one characteristic they all share irrespective of their backgrounds is their insatiable desire to always be learning. Being a chronic student enables you to ask, listen, learn, and inspire.

Chapter Eight: Everyone Has a Dream

Just as everyone has a story, everyone also has a dream. *Being the Real Deal* means as a leader you enable others to achieve their dreams. Turning dreams into reality is the ultimate leadership effectiveness measure. Never give up on the dream of equality, freedom, and justice. Never give up on the dream of creating a better world for all. Never give up on being an inspired and inspiring leader who leads with integrity.

Hope inspires us. We are better humans when we connect for the common good from a place of honesty, humility and caring for our fellow human beings. Make no mistake: Our moral fiber is in danger.

I do not believe our challenges are bigger than we are. We can raise standards for leaders. We can grow. I believe there is a leader in each of us that can and must make a positive difference in profound ways to address the multitude of challenges we all face. Yes, we can be inspiring leaders who promote freedom, justice, and equality.

Keep Growing!

Developing as a leader starts from the inside out. At the end of each chapter are questions to help you keep growing as a leader. One of my goals in writing this book is to have you ask the right leadership questions of yourself and others—not to give you the "right" answers. Do you want to learn how you show up in the eyes of all the people that matter to you? Are you rooted in the values that make you an authentic, ethical person?

Have you honestly assessed yourself and asked yourself and others about your effectiveness as a leader? What changes do you need to make? What are your strengths? What is your Achilles' heel as a leader?

Look at yourself before focusing your efforts on changing others. Why? If you want to improve your career, job, family, team, company, or community, the improvement must first "take root" in you. Choose to make a positive difference in every opportunity, no matter how big or small.

Are you showing up, speaking up and stepping up with integrity to make our world better in both small and big ways? As you read, my hope is you are inspired to make a positive difference. I ask you to cultivate an insatiable appetite for learning. Apply what you learn to yourself and become a more inspiring leader rooted in integrity who makes our world better for all by *Being the Real Deal.*

CHAPTER ONE

Leading With Mud on Your Shoes

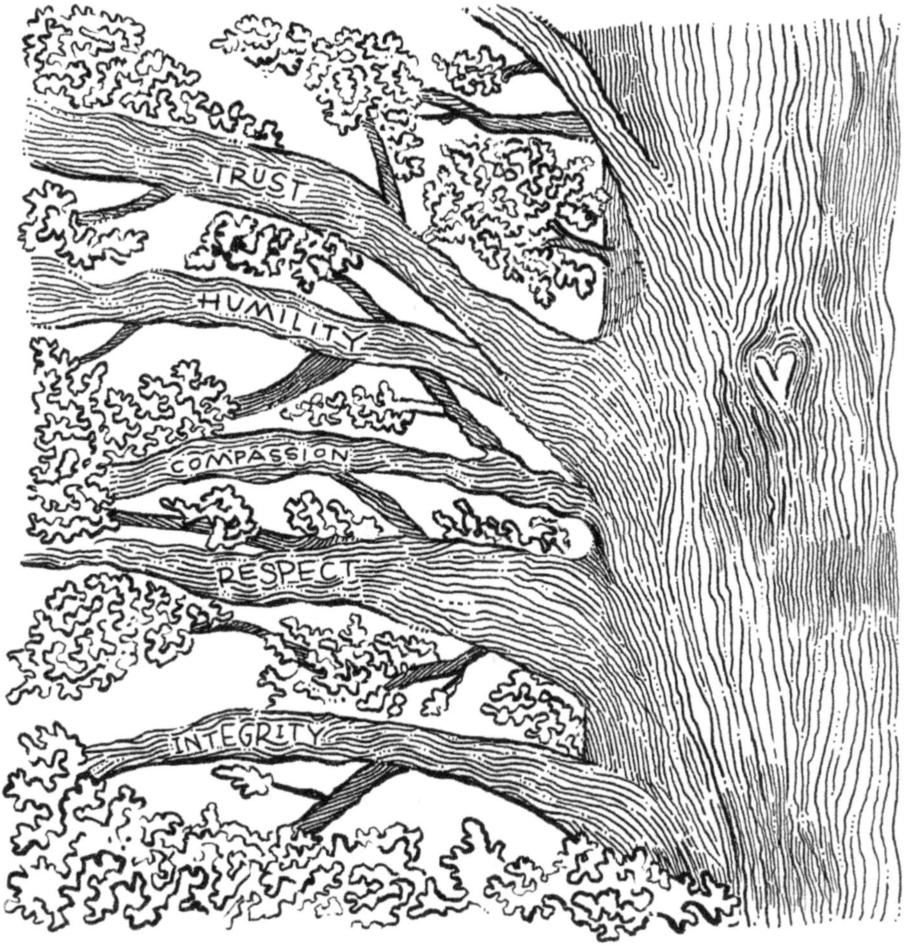

"Your visible values are what inspire other people to follow no matter what challenges you face."[1]

~ DAVID SPEER ~

Chairman and CEO of Illinois Tool Works, Inc.,

2006–2012

Visible Values Inspire

It was the summer of 2008. On a blue-sky morning, I drove from Chicago to Glenview, Illinois, to be interviewed for an incredible coaching opportunity. Illinois Tool Works (ITW), a 100-year-old global Fortune 500 manufacturing company, was developing its first formal global leadership development process. David Speer, the Chairman and CEO, was interviewing people to serve as his leadership coach.

Thrilled to have the opportunity, I braced myself for possible rejection. Being the token woman to be interviewed had become an all-too-familiar experience in the highly competitive C-suite coaching and consulting business. Even though I had significant experience working with CEOs and senior executives, women were scarce in the C-suite, especially in male-dominated industries like manufacturing. As the female founder of a small boutique consulting firm, I was a long shot compared to big-name male-led firms that surely were my competition.

In the middle of our interview, David Speer shocked me. He looked directly into my eyes and said, "Dr. Gordon, you're hired, let's get to work!"

Why shocked? David was renowned in the Chicago business and philanthropic community as well as globally as an outstanding leader. This meant one of the most respected global CEOs in business had chosen me—a female entrepreneur—as his leadership coach.

WOW—what a powerful equality message sent to all. I learned this was how David led. Change started with him and was initiated by his actions. Yes—David's visible values were firmly rooted. Leading meant embodying the changes he would set as expectations for others. He not only hired me as his leadership coach, he also recently hired two senior women as direct reports.

Without saying a word, David ensured women had seats at the decision-making table alongside the men reporting to him. David's leadership actions signaled diversity and inclusion as priorities. ITW's formal global diversity and inclusion process would soon follow.

Little did I realize our work together would be a once-in-a-lifetime coaching experience. David Speer was already an inspiring leader. He set the leadership bar high for himself. He was always willing to do the hard work first before asking the same of others. He embodied his values in his day-to-day work with passion and purpose. My experience working with David demonstrated to me once again a key to inspiring others is to make your values visible through your daily actions.

David also demonstrated the power of a leader's behaviors. Leading as the example rooted in integrity was David's job as CEO.

"Example is not the main thing in influencing others, it is the only thing."[2]

~ ALBERT SCHWEITZER ~

As Chairman and CEO, David Speer embodied the values needed to inspire others to meet any challenge then and now. His love for ITW—its people, customers, business model and values (especially ITW's strong commitment to the community)—was visible every day.

"David began his ITW career in 1978 as a marketing manager rising through the ranks to become the CEO in 2005 and Chairman of the Board in 2006. He was open to people at every level. It didn't matter whether you were a janitor or a CEO. People ended up trusting him."[3]
~ Jim Farrell, former ITW Chairman and the CEO
who hired David ~

As part of my ongoing leadership research, I interviewed David and asked, "What do you see as the challenges facing current and future CEOs?" He answered:

"I think you've got to reach out more and you've got to find more ways to engage people. [. . .] As I like to say to our people, you've got to get mud on your shoes! I use that analogy as I came up through the construction side of this business. You know, you learned what was going on in the construction business by standing on the job site in the mud next to the contractor."[4]

David knew the power of firsthand information by getting lots of "mud on his shoes" while directly engaging others. He also knew the power of his leadership to inspire innovation. David was a bold and courageous business leader who intuitively understood how ITW had to transform itself while retaining the values that made it successful.

"During his years as CEO, revenue grew about 40 percent, to an estimated $18.2 billion, but earnings were erratic, reflecting recessionary times. After falling 50 percent, net income rebounded to a record $2.1 billion in 2011. Meanwhile, ITW stock outperformed the broader market while Mr. Speer was CEO, rising more

than 60 percent (through mid-October) versus 30-some percent for both the S&P 500 Index and S&P 500 Industrials Index."[5]
~ Crain's Chicago Business, 2012 ~

David Speer is a great example of someone who lived the visible values of inspirational leadership. In addition to caring deeply about the success of ITW and all its employees, David was involved in numerous philanthropic pursuits. He saw his leadership role as being bigger than just one company, it extended to the Chicago community and throughout the world.

David was engaged and committed to community service, whether it was in Junior Achievement, the United Way, serving as Chairman of the Economic Club of Chicago, serving on the Boards of Northwestern University or the Museum of Science and Industry. David made a difference in the business and civic community with his active participation and leading with "mud on his shoes."

David loved ITW and his civic work, but he loved his family even more. Earlier in his career, despite a global travel schedule and heavy demands, he coached his son's baseball team and attended his daughter's swimming meets. Nothing brought a bigger smile than his time with his new grandson. Family was important, and time spent being truly present was not sacrificed.

By any measure—business, community and family—David Speer was a success.

Illinois Tool Works (ITW)

In 2008, ITW had over 875 decentralized business units in 54 countries employing 65,000 employees with annual revenue for 2008 of 15.9 billion.[6]

*"A tree can only be as strong as the forest that surrounds it . . .
their well-being depends on their community."*[7]

~ PETER WOHLLEBEN ~
The Hidden Life of Trees

All organizations profess to live by their business model and values. Yet few are as consistently successful as ITW at truly living its business model, processes and values in their day-to-day work. Each of the business processes and values listed below is woven into ITW's work fabric throughout the globe. They are not simply words on a glossy page in their annual reports. They are real.

ITW's Core Business Practices and Values

Decentralized entrepreneurial culture: "Decentralization is a core attribute of ITW . . . enabling them to act nimbly, seize opportunities, and adapt in response to market conditions."[8]

80/20 business process: "ITW's proprietary 80/20 business process has been integral to the company's success for nearly 30 years. Through the implementation of this process, each ITW business focuses on the 20 percent of its customers that generate 80 percent of its revenues and structures the business around serving and growing relationships with these key customers."[9]

Innovation: "Consistently recognized as a leading product innovator, ITW had over 21,000 patents and patent applications in 2008."[10]

Mutual trust & shared risk culture: David Speer, Chairman and CEO, explained, "In our environment, we talk openly about trust, integrity, and shared risk and those really embody the way we operate in the business every day. You have to have people that you trust and respect. Shared risk means I'm not asking you to take individual risk. We're going to take risk as an organization, as a team and we are going to work together."[11]

Leading During a Global Crisis:
The 2008—2009 Great Recession

As I talked with business leaders in late 2008, most saw one thing on the horizon: an economic downturn. However, the depth and breadth of the economic downturn was an unwelcome global surprise. The Great Recession was a leadership crucible for all. "On September 15, 2008, Lehman Brothers went under.[12] "The Federal Reserve and the United States Treasury nationalized the country's largest mortgage entities, Fannie Mae and Freddie Mac, who took over the world's largest insurance company, AIG."[13]

The housing market bubble burst and unprecedented actions sent shockwaves through global financial markets. The recession went spiraling out of control. Every day saw more bad news. The river of red ink just kept rising with no end in sight.

When would the worst global economic situation since The Great Depression be over? No one would venture a guess. Credit investments by businesses and consumers dried up. The U.S. labor market lost 8.4 million jobs.[14] These were dark days for all, as leaders faced painful decisions on how to stabilize and save their businesses and organizations.

How leaders act during crises magnify their values, making their values inescapably visible. A leader's visible values can inspire us to join together. Visible values can engage us to do the heavy lifting required to meet the challenges we face together. A leader's visible values can also divide and frighten us. Leaders can fail us by creating an "us versus them" dangerous game of survival where there are only winners and losers. Unbridled fear can be created by leaders who only care about themselves and their personal well-being.

As panic on Wall Street quickly spread to Main Street, no one was exempt from the pain. The horrors of the Great Depression were well known. Fear ran rampant throughout workplaces and boardrooms. The harsh economic realities created mass anxiety about job and organizational survival. The 2009 Great Recession tested every leader's mettle.

Leaders need the courage to stay true to their values in difficult times. David's leadership inspired others during this crisis. David Speer lived the visible values of inspirational leadership rooted in integrity. Now more than ever, we need leaders whose actions are rooted in honesty. We need leaders who inspire us because of their absolute integrity.

Instead of the panicked reaction of so many leaders slashing budgets and immediately laying off workers, David Speer stayed rooted in integrity and humility. When there's a crisis, the temptation for leaders is to revert to the old leadership paradigm of command and control—not David. Rallying his team around ITW's Core Business Processes and Values, he engaged teams in strategic decision-making to ensure ITW's long-term health financially and culturally. ITW's strengths—its values—were the guide rails for David and the company in meeting a global financial crisis not of their making.

David instinctively knew his leadership behaviors—his visible values—were his greatest tool for leading the company through these turbulent times.

"David had a steady hand at the helm. Some of our businesses lost half of their revenue overnight. They had to restructure at a pace and to an extent they never had to before. David was calm, cool and collected. He didn't panic. He coached people through the thought process around the restructuring issues."[15]
~ Sharon Brady, former SVP Human Resources, ITW ~

The courage to stay true to your values in a global economic crisis takes guts. The benefits of acting in line with your values in a time of crisis far outweigh the short-term gains of knee-jerk reactions.

Had David dictated decisions instead of coaching leaders, he would have destroyed the decentralized business model—a hallmark of ITW's success. Mutual trust and shared risk-taking would be only an ideal, not the reality on the ground. Once trust is destroyed in a leader, building trust back requires time, hard work, and confession of past failures. Relying on ITW's strengths, David built trust and respect by having ITW's values on display each day.

ITW rebounded from a 50-percent drop in net income to 2.1 billion in 2011. This was possible because David had earned the trust of all. Employees were treated with respect and dignity as valued team members. Communication was open and honest—yes, the unvarnished truth.

As the first cuts in jobs at corporate headquarters in the company's history were planned, David set up a confidential question box allowing any employee to submit a question to be answered in person during an all-hands meeting about ITW's business challenges and the needed job cuts. Lots of questions about the business, and some personal questions about David and senior leadership, filled the question box.

When asked, "Do you want to limit the number of questions answered during the employee meeting?" David roared back, "No matter how difficult or how many—every question submitted will be read and answered by me and members of senior leadership. Every person who took the time to submit a question deserves an honest, direct answer in public in front of their colleagues."

There would be no sugarcoating or dodging the painful reality all were experiencing. Corporate headquarters was being asked to do exactly what all the businesses were asked. David and his leadership team demonstrated in the meeting that day mutual trust and shared risk—the visible values being demonstrated at ITW businesses around the globe.

Our Coaching Partnership

As he came out of his office door, David would announce for all to hear he was meeting with his coach. Then with his never-ending supply of energy, he would burst into his conference room next door ready to engage in lively and candid discussion, debate and collaboration. We learned from and with each other. In the truest sense, we were partners in the leadership coaching effort. Yes, there was a formal process of goal setting, assessment with 360 feedback, individual development, and coaching plans, with regular monthly coaching sessions. However, we also worked real-time, with calls and emails, in the moment—like jazz musicians, listening to each other and improvising and building on each other's insights.

Raising the bar on his own leadership performance was a natural instinct for David. By doing so, he inspired others to raise the bar on their performance, including me. David appreciated hard work and forgave honest failures. But make no mistake, David Speer was all about results. There was never a time during our years of work together I did not feel challenged, inspired and appreciated.

The partnership formed with a leader makes or breaks any transformation effort—individual, team or organizational. Absolute trust, unvarnished honesty, a unity of purpose, passion and leaving egos at the door are all required. It's not just a matter of business—the partnership is caring, personal and real. When you have a connection of minds and hearts with each other, then and only then are you partnering.

David and I had the same purpose and passion for our work together. Raise leadership capabilities, and you raise the company's long-term success. David believed by setting the example of raising the bar on his own leadership effectiveness and that of his direct report team, he was planting the seeds for company-wide leadership development. He often said to me and to many others, "If the change takes root in me and those

I work most closely with, then I do not have to worry about the change taking hold in ITW's over 800-plus businesses around the globe—it will happen."

David led by example in the leadership development effort as he did in all aspects of ITW's business. Here was the CEO and Chairman of a global giant, and yet he wrote his own speeches. As he explained to me, "Why wouldn't I write my own speeches? I am giving the speech—shouldn't they be my words and not someone else's?" Classic David Speer—he was always leading with "mud on his shoes."

David insisted on being the first to go through ITW's formal global leadership development and coaching process. When I would introduce myself as David's leadership coach, many would say, "I didn't know David needed a coach—I mean, he is a great leader." This is the exact point David was making by having a public engagement with a coach: Even a great leader, even a CEO needs to continue to develop as a leader—you never stop learning as a leader.

David had all the business attributes one would want in a global CEO. He was strategic and operational with lots of "mud on his shoes." David showed no hesitation to stand and be truly seen as he openly shared his 360 feedback and development plan with his direct reports and the Board of Directors. He had the courage to be vulnerable. Transparency and humility made his vulnerability a strength.

David demonstrated his belief in the leadership and coaching process by experiencing it firsthand. His example of seeking feedback, using leadership development tools, and hands-on work with his direct reports was one more example of leading with "mud on his shoes."

David held me as his coach to the same high standard in delivering real-time value. Without hesitation he would say, "You got two out of three right, Vicky. Let's see if you can get three for three," always with an intense look and genuine smile on his face. When I asked for feedback on my coaching, David responded, "Believe me, if our work together was not adding value, I would not be spending this much time with you."

Time is a finite resource, and an 80/20 calendar evaluation of what David was spending his time on was conducted regularly with me and with his direct reports. Were you spending 80 percent of your time on your top priorities (your 20)? Time—a precious resource—was not to be wasted. However, David's sense of urgency to get things done never overrode his integrity and compassion.

Not a Check-the-Box Activity—a Genuine Leadership Learning Experience

David Speer was a larger-than-life personality. He commanded the energy in the room. We laughed, challenged, questioned, collaborated and learned together. He was fully engaged. This was not some process to go through and check the box. This was real self-reflection and analysis. Could he change himself and improve as a leader? Could he consistently demonstrate improvement to others? Could he become a better coach to his direct reports and have them grow as business leaders and as a team? To do this, he asked what he needed to improve and he listened. He shared his feedback and his development efforts.

When we discussed the coaching and development process, I remember him saying to me with his classic David Speer humor and passion: "Really Vicky, you mean the CEO still needs to develop as a leader? He doesn't know it all?" As David demonstrated, learning and growing as a leader is essential in every leadership position, starting with the CEO.

David was willing to be vulnerable by showing up authentically and revealing his feedback to his Board of Directors and his direct reports. This was one of the most powerful ways he could have his leadership development efforts take root. David shared his feedback and followed up. We measured his progress, and again David shared his feedback.

To be vulnerable in the moment requires courage and strength. David had both. Leading is not for the weak-kneed. Acts of courage are required each day to show your humanity and humility as you engage others to lead and be equally courageous.

David Speer's legacy is rooted in the example he set each day as a leader. Was he perfect? No, but he acknowledged his mistakes, never threw others under the bus, took responsibility, and never stopped learning. He engaged and inspired his fellow ITW colleagues and customers, his community, his friends, his family and his coach.

When I asked longtime ITW Board member Susan Crown to describe David as a leader for his first 360 feedback process, Susan said, "David is quite simply 'The Real Deal.'"[16] What is a leader who is The Real Deal? According to Susan Crown, a leader who is the real deal "does the right thing, in the right way, for the right reason."[17]

David's own words at the 2009 Lake Forest School of Management Commencement Speech demonstrate why Susan and others experienced David as *The Real Deal*.

*"If you can remember only one message from my remarks today—remember strong value-based leadership is one of the keys to your success. Values that are rooted in **trust and respect** for those you work with and those you serve, rooted in **integrity**. Always do what is right no matter what the personal consequences. Rooted in **humility** and the ability to admit your mistakes and allow others to make mistakes. Some of life's greatest lessons are learned from your mistakes. Rooted in **inspiration** and the ability to motivate and inspire people to work together and to do their very best. Rooted in **compassion** taking the time to understand the issues facing your people and how you can genuinely help them. Remember authority is given but leadership must be earned. Your visible values are what inspire other people to follow no matter what challenges you face."*[18]

"Try not to become a man (person) of success, but rather a man (person) of value."[19]

~ ALBERT EINSTEIN ~

David Speer was a person of true value. Day in and day out, regardless of challenges, he was quite simply always *Being the Real Deal.*

In April 2011, ITW announced David Speer was undergoing treatment for a medical condition. Like everything David did, this announcement was handled by the book. Sharon Brady, Senior VP of HR at the time, reached out to me as the news was hitting the press. David had asked Sharon to let me know the news but nothing else. David and I were scheduled for our regular coaching session that week, which Sharon asked to reschedule.

I wrote David an email that day, not knowing the health challenge he faced. I told him he and his family were in my prayers. I asked if I could do absolutely anything to be of support. I uncharacteristically signed it, "Your coach and friend, Vicky." Within an hour I received a reply from David. He thanked me for my support and said when "things calmed down" we would get together to resume our work together. He signed it, "Your student and friend, David." His response showed humility and caring for others even in a time of personal challenge. David's response still brings tears to my eyes.

Things never calmed down. We both knew time with his family and his beloved ITW family must be his priorities. We stayed connected via email, and he shared pictures of his grandson's first birthday with me. On November 17, 2012, David Speer lost his hardest-fought challenge. He left this world a better place because he led with his visible values and lots and lots of "mud on his shoes."

David left us too soon, but his legacy—his visible values rooted in trust, respect, integrity, humility, compassion and inspiration—continue to be experienced daily. *Being the Real Deal* lives on in Chicago at the ITW David Speer Academy founded in his memory, where future leaders learn to inspire others by visibly living their values. And all around the globe, ITW employees continue to learn and grow as leaders because leading with visible values with "mud on your shoes" took root.

Keep Growing!

1. How do others describe you as a leader?

2. What values are most visible to others in your daily leadership behaviors?

3. What specific behaviors can you do to be more inspiring?

4. How can you show more humility and compassion when leading? What are you doing to "earn" more respect from those you lead?

5. If you started leading with more "mud on your shoes," what story would you tell consistently?

"Character is like a tree and reputation like its shadow. The shadow is what we think of it; the tree is the real thing." [20]

~ ABRAHAM LINCOLN ~

16th President of the United States of America (1861–1865)

CHAPTER TWO

Everyone Has a Story

"Every great oak was once a little nut that held its ground."[1]

~ OLD ENGLISH PROVERB ~

Owning My Story

Have you ever walked barefoot through a freshly plowed field on a warm sunny spring day? The feel of the soft, warm, black earth squishing between my toes as I chased after my father on his Farmall Super A tractor is one of my favorite childhood memories.

Feeling the hardened winter dirt magically transforming into nurturing soil, ready for new crops signaled: **Planting Time!** Sinking ankle-deep into the rich ground, always on the lookout for an occasional earthworm fit for fishing later, I was connected to Mother Earth's most nurturing, fertile soil. Remembering the smell of freshly plowed dirt evokes in me a joyful feeling of connection to my family's farm.

My parents, Vivian Perry Gordon and Oscar Roland Gordon, were born into farming families and raised in rural North Carolina. Children of the Great Depression, they both knew what being poor meant, especially my dad. Mom's family (the Perrys) owned their farm. Dad's family (the Gordons) lived as sharecroppers. A 3-room wooden house with no running water, a well, and an outhouse was where Dad grew up. Dad, his eight siblings and my grandparents sharecropped on the Coley Arnold farm.

My parents saved money by my dad working in construction and by living in a small trailer for 10 years before having children. They eventually purchased the Coley Arnold farm, which became known as the Gordon homeplace—the farm where my lifelong values took root.

Being "raised" on a farm meant *working*. If you were old enough to walk, you were old enough to work on the farm. I raised chickens and sold the eggs to local grocery stores (my first business). My brother raised pigs for sale. We both saved the money we made for attending college. Strangely, neither of us was encouraged to become farmers. We always knew we would go to college to learn a different career. We were to have a better life than the back-breaking risky business of being a "dirt farmer."

The goal, though never spoken, was to do better than our parents. We were to get a better education and find a more lucrative profession. However, we were also to "never get above our raising." Our roots run deep as part of the land and the down-to-earth farm values my parents exemplified daily. My parents loved both of us equally. They sacrificed for us. They always put my brother and my needs ahead of their own.

Planting big gardens, achieving a bumper tobacco crop, my mother catching a big mouth bass at our pond just in time for dinner, fresh eggs for breakfast—yes, we were the original farm-to-table. These were the daily joys of growing up on our farm. I remember feeling sorry for people who had to buy food at the grocery store and eat "store-bought" food.

Later in life, when living in downtown Chicago, working in academia and corporate America, I missed the joys of farming. In my heart and soul, I am a farmer. The proud daughter of "dirt farmer" parents who sacrificed to give her the opportunities they missed. No matter where life takes me, my feet are always firmly grounded in our farm's rich black dirt near a branch of the Little River in North Carolina.

My parents planted the seeds to take root for my core values: **Integrity, Work Ethic, Humility, Love of Learning** and **Courage**. These are the roots keeping me grounded through good times and bad.

Integrity is Everything 

* Your word is your bond. If you promised to do something, then do it and do it to the best of your abilities.

* Honesty is always the best policy.

* All you have in life is your name—your reputation—do not let anyone tarnish it.

* Say what you mean and mean what you say.

* Always do the right thing for the right reasons, even if no one else will ever know.

* Lying, cheating, and stealing are wrong and not to be tolerated in small or large matters. If you lie about small things, you will lie about big things.

The most critical character trait for a person is honesty. Speaking the truth is deeply rooted in me by my parents. I remember my parents talking about others, "he is as honest as the day is long" or "he is a lying SOB—stay away from him and his friends. Birds of a feather flock together—you do not want to be seen with them." Roland and Vivian had absolute clarity on truth-telling. Right was right and wrong was wrong.

Honesty is the essential behavior for inspiring others. Sounds simple, but we are tested every day and in every stage of our lives. What I learned is, trust is an outcome of being honest. What you do and don't do—how you show up, speak up and step up creates your reputation. Your credibility rooted in your integrity is always on display—it's your invisible resume.[2]

Work Ethic 

* If you work hard enough, you can accomplish anything.

* If something is worth doing, it's worth doing well.

* Lazy is a four-letter word. Whatever the situation, one did not want to be seen as lazy and not doing quality work. If you took shortcuts and failed to get the work done right the first time, you would be sent back to do the work all over again. No matter how long and hard you must work, quality is never sacrificed.

Susan Crown, Chairman and Founder of SCE, listed work ethic as one of the essential behaviors making a leader The Real Deal for her. "You put everything you've got into what you are trying to achieve. You work really, really hard."[3] Exuding positive energy fueled by passion and a higher purpose inspires others to put their heart, mind and muscle into a common vision.

Dad was known for being able to "plow the mule down," a Southern saying meaning the mule would fall over from exhaustion while Dad would still be going strong. There were few if any who could claim this distinction. Working hard, putting in the time and effort, resilience, trying harder after failure, and never giving up once the goal is set is simply part of my DNA. The promise I could achieve anything if I just worked hard enough was drilled into my core.

My capacity for work is one of my greatest strengths. However, my over-reliance on this strength is also one of my greatest weaknesses. I burn out regularly. I even find myself working hard at relaxing. I am not alone in experiencing burnout. During the recent global Covid-19 pandemic people from all walks of life exhausted themselves with family, work, health, and safety. Just keeping food on the table was an overwhelming task.

A global CFO client once told me when maxed out "I am over-functioning." Stress, overworking, and unhealthy coping mechanisms are the downsides of "plowing the mule down." Reflection, rest, mindfulness, and self-care were not part of my hard-work mantra. As my son admonishes me still, "Mom, you just need to learn how to chill."

Don't work yourself to death, burning yourself out as you proudly "plow the mule down." Remember: *Leading is a marathon, not a sprint.*

Humility 

* "You are not better than anyone else and no one is better than you," Dad admonished us. "Everyone puts his or her britches on the same way—one leg at a time."

* Always give a helping hand to those in need. *"If you have done this for the least of them then you have done this for me."*[4]

* Treat everyone with the same respect.

* "Never get above your raising."

* Admit your mistakes and learn from them. "Only people who don't do anything don't make mistakes," according to my dad. "Be proud of trying, learn and then try again." There is no shame in failing, shame is reserved for *not* trying.

I did not know what "Never get above your raising" meant when I was a small child, but I learned quickly. Acting like someone who thought they were more successful and better than others because they had more money was wrong. My dad was adamant: "I do not want to go to anyone's house where I cannot 'saucer my coffee,'"[5] which means where he cannot be himself. Acting like you were better than other folks for any reason or pretending to be someone you are not represent major character flaws.

Love of Learning 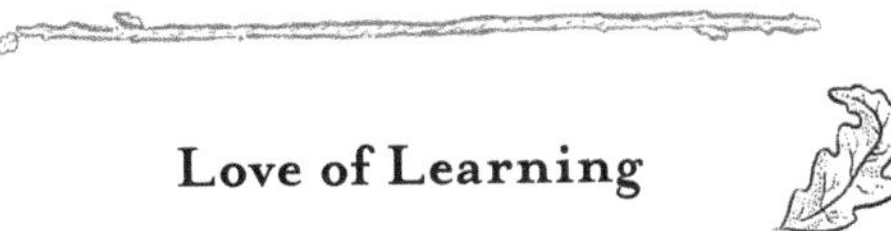

* People can take away everything you own, but if you learn something, it's yours forever.

* "Book" learning and "practical" experience are both needed and equal in value.

* Crave knowledge and understanding, the facts, the truth, and treasure your ability to learn something new every day. Learning is the lifeblood of successful living.

Learning how to plant vegetables, say multiplication tables from memory backward, change the tires on my 1961 Chevy Impala or recite long passages from the King James Version of the Bible are a few of the cherished things I learned from my parents.

Why the love of learning? Dad had to stop school after 4th grade to go to work, and Mom attended high school but did not graduate. Neither of my parents were given the gift of a "book learning" education. They both wanted the best education possible for their children, whether "book learning" or how to do things. My parents believed learning was essential for a better life. Thanks to my parents I became a "chronic student" who loves learning in all its forms.

December 9, 1977, I talked on the phone from Austin, Texas, with Dad in North Carolina. It was my first semester working on my Ph. D. at the University of Texas at Austin. I asked him, "How does Dr. Gordon sound to you, Pop?" He answered, "Dr. Gordon sounds great!" Two days later, my father died in his sleep from a massive heart attack. Every time I see or hear myself referred to as Dr. Gordon, I know it's a shout-out to Dad and Mom. Well done; your daughter achieved the first Ph. D. in our family.

Courage

* Take risks. Dad never allowed me to say, "I can't." He insisted, "Can't never did do nothing. Go ahead and try."

* If you fail, pick yourself up, dust yourself off, and go at it again with more fire in your belly, passion and hard work.

* Never give up. Be resilient. "Where there is breath there is hope," advised my grandma Nannie Lou Bunn Perry who encouraged all in difficult times.

Farming, by its nature, requires courage and resilience. Every year, there is a possibility of flooding or drought. Every year, my parents went into debt in the hopes of making a profit. Every year, they would take that leap of faith and risk everything to survive and thrive.

I learned by example from my first teachers: my parents. No matter what the role—student, teacher, scholar, organizational development consultant, entrepreneur, team builder, leadership coach, wife, mom, daughter, sister, caregiver, or friend—my joy comes from cultivating, planting, growing, improving, changing myself for the better. Helping others bloom and blossom is an even greater joy. What I love about my work is engaging with individuals, teams and organizations, enabling others to grow to be their best.

"There is no greater agony than bearing an untold story inside you." [6]

~ DR. MAYA ANGELOU ~
I Know Why the Caged Bird Sings

Owning and sharing my story has been a painful struggle for me. Shame can be a powerful block to our willingness to share our stories. Hearing stories from so many brave women who have gone before me and on whose shoulders I stand gives me courage. No, I can no longer pretend the cultures of abuse and discrimination have not touched me. Honestly, it would be so much easier for me to leave my story out of this book, but it would not be honest. *Being the Real Deal* requires honesty, vulnerability, and courage. Owning my story and telling it to others is part of me *Being the Real Deal.*

Creating a brand is easy—creating an honest brand requires guts. Pulling weeds and digging deep is hard work. Destroying what does not serve you anymore creates vulnerability. However, nothing grows to its full potential unless one is willing to weed out old negative patterns and experiences stunting one's growth. Light is required for growth.

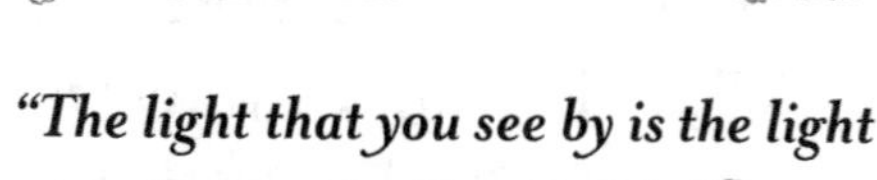

"The light that you see by is the light that comes from inside."[7]

~ THE RADIANCE SUTRAS ~

My Hidden Story

Underneath. Hidden from sight. Deep scars. Old wounds and suffering brought on by others have a way of coming to the surface despite a lifetime of blessings. So it is with me. After years of feeling deep shame, I understand why I created masks to distance myself from even the people who love me the most. On that same rich soil were planted some poisonous seeds. Only after years of therapy do I have the courage to speak the truth—to myself, my therapist, my loved ones, and now to you.

Not Good Enough Seed

Discrimination because we were "dirt farmers" was never openly discussed in my family. Unexplained discrimination in a small-town culture existed. White folks who lived in town in brick houses and had "professional" jobs as bank president, dentist, and insurance agent were somehow "better" than the White folks living in the country working in the fields less than three miles away.

We were not "good enough" because Dad and Mom were "dirt farmers." Dad wore bib overalls and his false teeth stayed on the shelf in the kitchen cabinet more than in his mouth. I didn't know the term for it then, but I felt discrimination as a child.

The discrimination I experienced as the daughter of a farming family was more than just a feeling. In the 3rd grade, I was placed in a different classroom from my best friend because she lived in town, and I lived in the country. I felt like I was being punished. The separation just hurt my heart. What had I done wrong? Was I not good enough to be in the same class as all the town kids?

The explanation given to my mom was, "Getting children on the school bus was quicker if all those living in the country were in the same 3rd-grade classroom." Mom knew the truth because she had experienced this truth her entire life. Mom had me moved to the "town group," and the separation of town kids and country kids did not happen again while we were growing up.

Mom made certain we did all the things the town folks did. We went to the church in town, not the country church. We took dance classes, swimming lessons, piano lessons, and were in Boy Scouts and Brownie Scouts. Mom joined a bridge club in town, and Dad volunteered for the Booster Club supporting school athletic activities. My brother was the school football hero, and I was in the marching band.

Even so, we still experienced class discrimination, like not being invited to the "in-town" birthday parties or other social engagements. The repeated exclusion left its mark. I began to internalize the feeling of not being "good enough." I felt like my "slip was showing": My clothes, my hair, and our home did not match up to those of "town girls."

I never felt as smart, pretty, or confident as the girls who lived in town seemed. Even as I moved on to college, I experienced imposter syndrome, wondering how a dirt farmer's daughter could ever be equal to my mostly tall, blonde, and wealthy sorority sisters at the University of North Carolina at Chapel Hill.

My entire educational and professional life has been fueled by proving and showing them Dad and Mom were good enough, my family was good enough, and, dammit, I am good enough. Given the discrimination I felt (and we were "respectable White folks" in the early 1960s), I learned firsthand how devastatingly hurtful discrimination is to a child, a parent, a family, a community, and all of us.

"Black folks" in the segregated South of my childhood were lynched, crosses burned in their yards and denied basic human dignity. I cannot imagine the pain and the scars of racial discrimination Black Americans live with every day. Today, the racial justice struggles of the 1960s continue in 2024. If I close my eyes, it seems it's the 1960s in America. I remember Whites-only water fountains, I remember being in all-White classrooms. I also remember attending William G. Enloe High School—the first integrated high school in Raleigh. I remember sitting in a classroom with African American students for the first time. What I experienced—*not good enough*—is not even on the same planet as the continued systemic racism and discrimination of Black and Brown Americans.

I have zero tolerance for discrimination of any kind. The bad seed did not take root; instead, the seed of equality for all, showing respect for all human beings is my deeply held conviction. Black Lives Matter. Standing against discrimination and standing for equality must be actions, not just words. Will you call out family, friends, and colleagues for racism and all forms of discrimination? Yes, you must! Yes, I have and will continue to do so until I take my last breath!

"Don't allow anybody to make you feel that you're nobody. Always feel that you count, that you have worth and that your life has ultimate significance."[8]

~ Dr. Martin Luther King, Jr. ~

I Am a Victor—Not a Victim

I was five years old. I was left in someone's care my parents trusted. The trauma took place on the dam overlooking the pond on our farm, which my dad said he had built just for me.

It is my deepest held secret, the "bad girl" seed, the experience that began a series of "badness"—like a chain reaction. People only saw me from the outside with no clue what had ignited the "bad behaviors" hidden so deep in my heart.

Shame I did not deserve came later when I learned what was done to me was wrong. I was a happy little 5-year-old ballerina when I was fondled and molested. Everyone thought it was so nice this young man enjoyed taking care of me. If they had only known—no doubt my father and mother would have beaten him to a pulp.

I was not kept safe. This innocent little girl was transformed into a fat, ugly adolescent, setting in place an entire series of "good girl," "bad girl" feelings and behaviors. I would do things like overeat, overdrink, overwork, and over-everything. Then I beat myself up psychologically for once again being a "bad girl" when my behaviors were self-sabotage and self-destructive. As I faced growing up and dealing with challenges everyone experiences, I started having symptoms of post-traumatic stress disorder (PTSD) that I did not understand until many years later.

No one knew about what had happened except myself and the young man who stole my childhood innocence. Why didn't I tell someone? Why didn't I run away or try to stop him from touching me? I remind myself I was told to obey him. I trusted him. My family trusted him. I did not know how to protect myself from anyone who tried to touch me "down there." I did not know how to keep myself safe.

The lack of safety created a hole in my heart that could not be filled. No matter how much I accomplished, or how much other people genuinely loved me, I did not feel loved because I never felt safe. They loved the "good girl" they saw on the outside, not the "bad girl" I knew I was on the inside. The ballerina turned into a fat but determined teenager who later transformed herself into a successful professional with all the trappings of "having it all."

I've struggled with major bouts of depression. Behaviors of "self-sabotage" and "bad girl" were planted deep inside me. It was hard to overcome the feeling of shame, no matter how much I worked or did. I didn't feel safe enough to feel the love that I am so blessed to have in my life. I experienced some of life's normal challenges as life-threatening events—triggering a fight, flight, or freeze response lasting days, months or even years. PTSD kept me on high alert.

Courage to Be Seen

It's taken years to have the courage to tell my story—to speak my truth. A pivotal first step for me was when I read Dr. Maya Angelou's *I Know Why the Caged Bird Sings*. I felt a deep connection with her and her story. I was blessed to meet her at a fundraiser for the Chicago Foundation for Women in 1994. At a private reception I co-hosted, I waited in line to be introduced and shake her hand.

As we reached to shake each other's hands, I looked into her eyes and said, "We have two things in common: I grew up in the South—North Carolina. I also know 'why the caged bird sings.'"[9] Tears started rolling down my cheeks. As only she could do, Dr. Maya Angelou read my soul that day. She gave me the most loving hug and said knowingly, "We are sister friends." At that moment, I knew I was not alone; another soul knew my pain.

My journey to being "wholehearted and worthy"[10] continues with the ongoing support and love of my husband Don, my many sister friends and my family.

Courage to be seen—totally seen—has taken me a lifetime. It is never too late to own your story. Remember: Voicing your story—your truth—enables others to have the courage to tell their stories, heal and grow.

Don't forget: It's never too late to plant a new seed—an acorn of your own choosing. You have the power to choose what needs rooting out and what gets planted.

I have deep love and gratitude for my husband, our son, my therapist shaman Doris, The 5 W Club, all my sister friends, mentors and my parents. I gained the courage to dig deep, pull the roots of the bad seeds out of the mud. As one of my favorite comedians Al Franken as Stuart Smalley says, "I am good enough, smart enough and doggone it . . . people like me."[11]

One acorn can grow into a powerful oak tree. One tiny acorn has the potential for greatness if it takes root and grows continuously throughout its life. We too can develop into great leaders regardless of our past, by doing the inspiring work of growing each day.

The hole in my heart is being filled. I feel safe to speak my story—my truth. Yes, I feel more blessed and grateful every day. I am excited to still be learning and growing. I continue to learn truths and wisdom from all my clients, colleagues, friends, and family. Yes, I feel grounded most days, but I am still a work in progress. Healing is an everyday practice of giving and receiving love. Learning to love myself with all my imperfections is still a challenge. I am passionate about sharing what I have learned about *Being the Real Deal* as an inspiring leader rooted in integrity.

I am *not* advocating you should bear your soul to the world. There is more to my story, but this is what I choose to share with the public. How and with whom you share your story is totally in your hands. Leadership strength through vulnerability comes in many forms. Always remember, *no one gets to define who you are—this is your right and yours alone.*

"The privilege of a lifetime is to become who you truly are."[12]

~ JOSEPH CAMPBELL ~

Keep Growing!

1. What values have taken root in you?

2. What is your truth?

3. How do you want to own your story more directly?

4. What is the story about you as a person you want to share that enables others to know the real you?

5. What is the story you want others to tell about you as a leader?

"Even when it's not pretty or perfect. Even when it's more real than you want it to be. Your story is what you have, what you will always have. It is something to own."[13]

~ MICHELLE OBAMA ~

Becoming

CHAPTER THREE

Either You Have It or You Don't

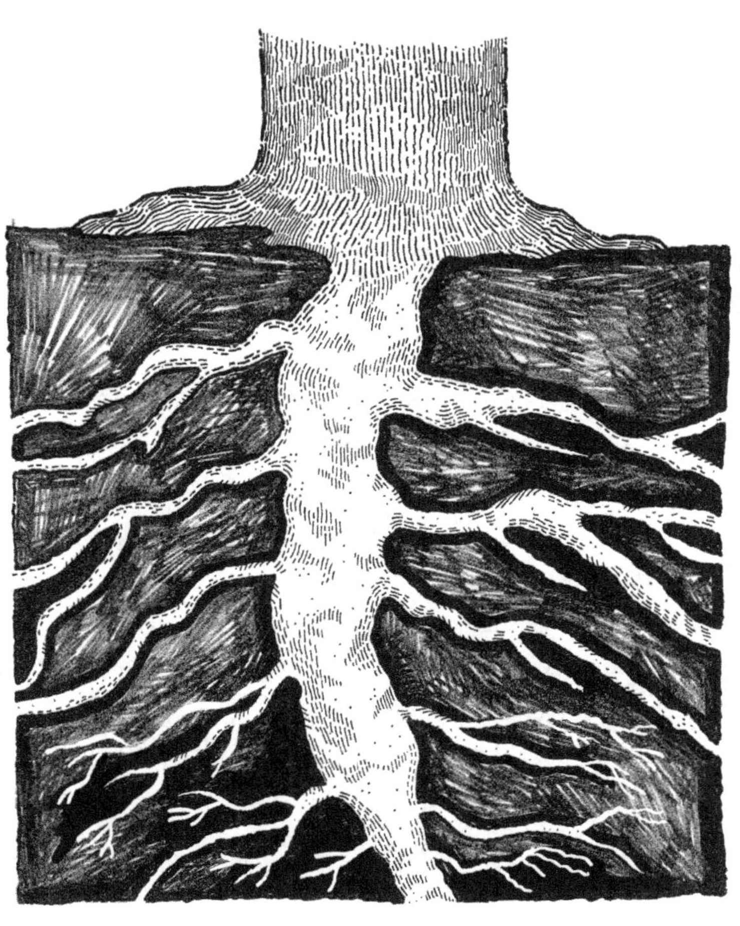

"An oak tree's tap root can grow up to 20 feet deep, making it one of the deepest tap roots of any tree. The tap root is the primary root that grows straight down from the tree's trunk. Most other roots branch out from the tap root. The tap root anchors the tree . . ."[1]

~ THE DEEPEST TAP ROOT: AN OAK TREE'S JOURNEY

MAST-PRODUCING-TREES.ORG ~

Integrity Is the Taproot of Leadership

The taproot is the oak tree's first anchor and provides nourishment for growth. So it is with integrity being the anchor from which we are taught how to lead as ethical people.

> *"West Point Cadet Code of Honor: A cadet will not lie, cheat, or steal, or tolerate those who do."*[2]

As a West Point graduate with a personal tradition of honorable leadership, my coaching client was genuinely excited to receive his 360 feedback. During our initial conversation, he made it clear he was eager to continue learning and growing.

Prior to my receiving his 360 feedback report, I spent an hour interviewing my client. He was clearly an accomplished senior executive. The last thing I was expecting to read in his feedback report was low ratings on integrity.

After reading his 360 feedback report, completed by his direct manager, peers, direct reports, and internal customers on his company's leadership competencies, he clearly had many strengths. Not surprisingly, he had rated himself highest on Integrity and Trust out of his company's 17 leadership competencies.

However, the feedback indicated one *enormous* blind spot. The feedback on integrity was going to be a hurtful surprise—a stab to his heart—a powerful punch in the gut. Given the person I had interviewed and his 5-star resume, I was baffled by the wide ratings disparity among those providing feedback on integrity and trust. There were no clear answers as to why some but not all had rated him low on integrity.

His direct manager had given him the highest rating possible on integrity. He received high marks for Courage and Drive for Results from all. However, some direct reports and peers rated Integrity and Trust low with a wide variance in ratings.

Here was an accomplished leader whose direct manager and self-assessment were highest on Integrity, but some saw this leader as radically different. "Many do not trust him," "My perception was positive in the beginning but decayed as time went on." Low ratings and tough words to hear about yourself. Our coaching meeting the next day was going to be challenging for both of us.

Integrity Through Others' Eyes

As we worked page by page through my client's detailed feedback report, there were initially no surprises. My client was his jovial self with the usual dose of sarcastic humor which we both enjoyed and understood.

My client read the quantitative results for each question and the open-ended comments at the end of each comment section. The feedback report was organized from the highest-rated to lowest-rated competencies. My hope was my client would internalize all the feedback about his strengths prior to the last page. Once we got to Integrity and Trust, I knew my client's ability to listen, digest and move forward might come to a screeching halt.

There in black and white—**Integrity and Trust**—ranked by others as second in importance of the 17 leadership competencies—and ranked lowest in my client's performance. I will never forget the look on his face when he saw the scores and read the comments.

My client turned red—a bright-red face and red ears—as he slumped down in the chair as if he had been shot directly in the chest. The pain was palpable. "Oh my God, I have never received anything but praise for my absolute integrity and honesty. This is devastating." Tears came to his eyes.

The biggest blind spot of his career was now revealed. How he dealt with it would be a turning point in his career. The silence between us was deafening. I did not want to rescue him from the feedback's reality. He had integrity and trust issues with segments of his peers and direct reports.

I broke the silence: "Remember, feedback is others' perceptions through their lenses—not right or wrong, but perceptions."

"Excuse me," he said and stood up, "I'm going to the bathroom. I need a few minutes."

"Okay, I will take a break as well and meet you back in the hallway."

Negative Feedback's Power

One of my greatest fears about sharing negative feedback is there are challenges going on in people's lives I have no way of knowing, even though I ask. Clients choose what they will disclose.

Business has for too long required people to leave their problems, humanity, blessings, and emotions at the company's front door. We should be able to bring our whole selves to our work. As Dr. Susan David puts it, "When we show up fully, with awareness and acceptance, even the worst demons usually back down."[3]

Before engaging in any feedback process, I assess how fragile the person and situation are. Can the person benefit from the "unvarnished truth" to grow as a leader? Many love learning and getting both positive and negative feedback. Some leaders crave honest, unfiltered perceptions of their leadership effectiveness. The more they learn from the feedback, the better.

Feedback affirming what we think of ourselves, and our intentions, gives us opportunities to focus our learning and development. But when it comes to learning about our blind spots—we are all fragile.

I remind people that feedback is a slice in time—a picture through other people's lenses. The 360 feedback process creates a collective perception picture. The 360 feedback is the narrative others are telling about your current leadership effectiveness—it is not right or wrong. Your assessment of yourself as a leader is equally important as is your intent, even if others question it.

Fact: There is no way to take the sting out of negative feedback, even when the person agrees with the feedback. Negative feedback is a thousand times more painful when your assessment of yourself does not come close to others' narrative of you.

The most painful feedback is when your integrity is questioned because you know you are honest and trustworthy. It is gut-wrenching when you pride yourself on being consistently honest and your character is questioned.

Integrity defined who my client was as a person. Absolutely he believed himself to be trustworthy and trusted. Telling the truth even when it's difficult was the standard operating practice in both his professional and personal life. Throughout my client's life integrity, trust, and credibility were absolute strengths. The principles and practices of integrity were just part of his DNA root system—growing from his taproot and spreading deep and wide throughout his life.

Integrity as a Blind Spot

As my client and I walked down the hallway back to our conference room, my mind raced ahead. Had denial set in? Was he angry? How do I help him acknowledge the hurt and move to acceptance of the feedback? What did the feedback mean? What was clear? What required clarification? How does he get a clearer understanding of the dynamics creating his low integrity and trust narrative with some and not with others? How does he turn sharing the feedback into a genuine effort to establish his integrity and build trust with all?

Clearly, opposite narratives had been constructed of this leader's behaviors. If not addressed, the lack of trust, honesty and integrity narrative could fester and grow. Without trust, a lack of teamwork could hurt the function and directly affect customers. Trust is an outcome built by others experiencing you as consistently transparent and honest. If you are perceived as lacking integrity, people will not trust what you say or do.

We had our work cut out for us to get to root causes with as little defensiveness as possible. Sitting back down, looking directly into my eyes, my client said, "So, Mrs. Lincoln, how did you like the play?" We both laughed at his typical use of sarcastic humor.

I responded, "It sucked."

"It certainly does suck," he responded.

I asked, "How do you explain the wide variance in the feedback?"

"I can't, I don't know. Honestly, I am still in shock. This just isn't who I am as a leader, and more importantly, this is not who I am as a person."

Then he said in all seriousness, "I guess the easiest thing to do to fix this is to find out all that scored me low and fire them."

With what must have been a look of total horror on my face, he quickly said, "I was kidding, you know my sarcastic sense of humor."

"I do, but do all the people on your team know when you are being sarcastic? Have you made jokes about firing people in jest?"

"Probably, but everyone knows I was kidding." The parts of the puzzle started emerging.

Highly analytical and an introvert, my client needed to think through information to understand it. He needed a way to start to internalize and think through how to surface more pieces of the puzzle. We started through a self-reflection process focused on the here and now—grounding him back into his current leadership business challenges.

As we talked, he hit a point where he just "let it rip," sharing all his frustrations and challenges. "I was new to the company. I was hired—I thought—to bring about cultural change. Drive for Results and getting things accomplished have been strengths throughout my career. Unfortunately, I inherited a tightly knit group of teams who were not just co-workers, but good friends.

"The second week I was here the company had its first layoff ever. I was ordered to downsize a specific number, which I did based on business needs. I told the truth and made some hard decisions." After three hours, my coaching client had gotten all the things off his chest over which he felt he had no control.

"The truth will set you free but first it will piss you off."[4]

~ GLORIA STEINEM ~

Feedback as a Trust-Building Tool

So the question became: How could this leader use his feedback to demonstrate to all his peers and direct reports that he is a leader and person of integrity? The first opportunity to start changing the honesty narrative was just outside the conference room where we were meeting. We were in an open office environment, where all knew he was getting his feedback that day. This gave many eyes and ears a chance to see and hear my client's initial reaction to his feedback. Transparency and honesty were essential. His verbal and nonverbal communication coming out of the meeting to his assistant, team members and peers would be the first step in changing the negative narrative about his truthfulness and trustworthiness—his integrity.

We discussed leaving our feedback meeting and his nonverbal and verbal communication. He needed a truthful narrative about the feedback he received. So when asked what his response was to his feedback, he said, "The feedback was candid and honest. I am grateful for the insights. Some parts were difficult to hear but all valid and important for me to understand." My client was genuinely upbeat and smiled as he left our meeting. His homework was to summarize his data into bullet points of strengths and weaknesses. We would reconvene the next morning.

Changing the Narrative—Honesty and Humility in Action

My client decided the only way to change perceptions was to be honest and humble. He did this by sharing all his feedback and listening deeply to individuals, so they felt heard. He learned why and how perceptions of his lack of integrity had been created in some people.

New to the company, my client had been 100 percent task-focused on delivering on what his manager had told him to do—without the benefit of having first established trusting relationships with some peers and direct reports. He also had failed to communicate why the layoffs were essential. Business needs were the sole drivers of his decisions. Technical competencies took priority over longevity. The total task-focused behaviors, combined with some taking his sarcastic humor seriously, explained how and why some perceived him as lacking integrity.

Sharing the "unvarnished truth" about his feedback demonstrated humility and a genuine desire to improve his leadership behaviors. He listened to understand in one-on-one meetings. His non-defensive questions elicited ways he could change to demonstrate through his leadership behaviors the fact that he is a person and leader with integrity.

My client established new, more open lines of communication with ongoing feedback to and from all. And now anytime he uses sarcastic humor, he remembers to say, I was joking. This leader's actions changed perceptions.

*"Integrity is your destiny—it is the light
that guides your way."*[5]

~ HERACLITUS ~

Do As I Say, Not As I Do

My clients simply expect me to get my services right the first time because their careers, reputations and the company's performance are on the line. They trust me to deliver on time and on budget, while producing concrete results. No one wants a series of activities without the desired outcomes. If you don't keep your word, your integrity takes a hit, and repeat business is unlikely.

Starting my organizational development consulting and leadership coaching business was exciting and challenging. We had completed developing a performance management process for a client. We had also been hired to implement the new performance management process by training all the organization's managers and employees. The organization's President was to send out a letter to all managers explaining what, why, when, and how the new performance management process would be implemented. My office was to write the President's letter and send it to my client for the President's signature and distribution.

Everyone in my office (including myself) proofread the letter so many times we could literally recite the letter line by line. We sent the letter to the client, Trisha, the Vice President of Employee Services, for the President to sign and send to all managers (yes, it was old school—a real letter).

The next day, I looked at the President's letter as I was cleaning my desk and my heart stopped—there was a *Typo*. "Oh *no!* How the hell did we miss this?" Then I asked my team, "How the hell did you all miss this?" In a total panic, I picked up the phone and called my client. It was too late; the letter had been sent out to managers. I panicked, thinking we would get fired because of this error, over making the President look bad and our work look even worse. Couldn't we even proofread?

I was falling on my sword with apologies over the phone to Trisha, our client, promising to make it right by sending out another letter at our expense, promising to do just about anything to make up for this single typo. Our work had not been perfect—and I was in full crisis mode.

Trisha (our client) said something to me that day I have never forgotten: "Calm down Vicky, no one died, it was a typo, it's not a crisis; fix it for the next letter going out to all employees."

Trisha taught me mistakes happen. Some are life-and-death, but most are not—the typo being one of them. To this day, I ask myself and my clients: If this does not work, or if you make a mistake, what happens? Will you lose the business? Will the patient die? Can you afford the learning curve?

If there is no room for error, then the process must have a fail-safe system every step of the way. For example, I took a group of students to a British manufacturing plant in England that makes pipes for North Sea oil drilling. The plant manager shared that in their contracts every pipe going out of the plant must be perfect. The risk of a pipe failure would be catastrophic for the environment and for the drilling company. They had lots of faulty pipes laying around, but only the perfect ones got shipped. The plant cannot make all pipes perfect, but it can make sure only the perfect pipes are shipped to its customers.

The real damage I did with my panicked reaction to a typo was to my relationship with my team. My integrity as their leader took a big hit. I was panicked—in full PTSD stress overload—cortisol had hijacked my prefrontal cortex and I was not thinking, just reacting. Here I was, behaving the way I coached other leaders not to behave. My integrity was damaged. I felt foolish and embarrassed. I had overreacted, treating a typo as if we had killed someone.

What did I learn about my leadership integrity from this mistake? First, I did the exact opposite of what I coach leaders to do. I was guilty of "Do as I say, not as I do." My words to clients and my actions with my own team were the opposite. Chastising people for making an honest mistake is irresponsible. I had thrown my team under the bus without me.

To correct the situation, I apologized and took personal responsibility as their team leader for missing the typo and for "losing my cool." I explained to the team how we (starting with me) had all missed the typo. I asked what we (starting with me) could do in the future to avoid the exact same mistake. We need to learn from our mistakes, not be punished for them. In the team meeting, I shared Dad's mantra:

"Only people who don't do anything don't make mistakes." [6]

~ OSCAR ROLAND GORDON ~

For my dad, "Your word was your bond." For him, all that was needed to do business was a handshake and your word to deliver on your commitments. The world is far different today: Honesty, integrity and trust are at an all-time low.

However, "your word" is still the litmus test for your professional and personal reputation for honesty. Speaking the truth in all situations is a measure of your integrity. If you make a mistake, take responsibility, and have the humility to learn from others what you can do better as a leader next time.

In all my years of client work, there is no one whose leadership behaviors are more inspiring to me because of their integrity and humility than Githesh Ramamurthy, Chairman and Chief Executive Officer of CCC Intelligent Solutions. His absolute integrity and humility are inspiring. I can hear Githesh asking, "Is there anything I could have done differently to prevent or solve this problem?"

Blessed to have worked with Githesh and CCCIS, there was never a situation in our work together where he did not question his own leadership behaviors before questioning others' leadership behaviors. People respect Githesh's brilliant innovative technology and business mind. However, people love working with Githesh because he leads with visible values of integrity and humility, even in the toughest situations. Chairman and CEO Ramamurthy is a leader who is always *Being the Real Deal.*

Are you known for honest communication in public and private? Do you treat all people with dignity and respect while taking responsibility? Do you invite candid feedback on all aspects of your leadership behaviors? Do you know the narrative others are telling about you?

**"Humility is not thinking less of yourself,
it's thinking of yourself less."** [7]

~ RICK WARREN ~

The Purpose Driven Life

Say It to My Face—Not Behind My Back

Mary was off-the-scale analytical. Few got past the barrage of questioning she would initiate at the beginning of every interaction. As I read her 360 feedback, I felt sad. No one liked working with her: She was "negative, rigid, critical of everything and all new ideas."

People literally dreaded seeing her name on a team list to have to work with her. Honestly, this was my first reaction to her as well. In our first coaching meeting, she challenged everything I said about the coaching process. The "grilling" made me feel like I did not want to have to argue with her for the next 12 months as her coach. Mary's direct manager shared his concern: "If Mary does not change and change soon, I do not know how much longer I can protect Mary from being fired."

Mary was highly valued for her technical expertise and analytical skills, but at what cost to the morale of the teams with which she worked? In the 40-page 360 feedback report I received from her fellow employees, there was only one comment giving insight as to who Mary truly was: "After 2 years of working closely with Mary, I recognized she is highly analytical and cares deeply about getting the task done right."

I thought to myself, Mary's total task focus and the impression she makes on people are so strong, it takes years for only one person to break through to the *real* Mary. Before she and I discussed the feedback, she confided in me: "The first impression I make with people has always been negative—and it's even taken my best friends years to get to know me and like me."

When I met with Mary for the first time, I experienced the same negative, critical energy. It was like the grand inquisition:

"I don't understand what you just said, Vicky, it doesn't seem logical. Can you give me data points supporting your statement?" By the end of the hour, I was ready to pull my hair out.

I decided to use our first meeting as a way for Mary to experience the effect of her behavior on others, so I delayed sharing the devastating data from her 360 feedback. I started by giving my assessment of our first meeting: "Working together was no fun—it wasn't enjoyable, and it felt like we made no progress at all."

Mary responded, "Work isn't supposed to be fun or enjoyable. We need to be efficient and get the job done." Crack the whip early and often seemed to be her leadership mantra. No one had the integrity and courage to share with her how her "crack the whip" behaviors had created an extremely negative reputation.

"Mary, did you ever consider if I dislike working with you, it will take five times as long to get the job done? What were you trying to achieve by grilling me on everything I said? Do you think you got to know the real me and I got to know the real you?"

We spent the next several meetings working real-time on taking the mask off, learning about each other, and about first impressions. Mary realized by letting people know the *real* Mary, people would see she could lead beyond just forcing data down their throats. Intellectually, she got it. She used the mask to protect herself because she was shy and afraid of making a mistake. In her male-dominated work environment, Mary felt she could not afford to make a mistake. Women were held to a higher standard. She felt she had to be perfect.

The adjectives peers used to describe Mary were painful for her to hear. "That's not really how I feel—it's not really me." Tears started streaming down her face. The first reaction to feedback not matching our own self-perception is usually defensive. Others' perceptions are wrong. Yet perceptions cannot be right or wrong—they are created by experiencing others' behaviors through personal, individual lenses.

You don't control other people's perceptions of your behaviors. You only control your own behavior. Mary's challenge was to enable people to get to know the real her—within 2 weeks instead of 2 years. Yet we all know first impressions are powerful and difficult to change once established. This would have to be a total turnaround for Mary. She needed to reframe her well-established brand of being "a pain in the ass." Mary's brand needed to become one where people wanted her on their team and genuinely enjoyed working with her to achieve great results.

Mary decided her development goal was to make working with her energizing and enjoyable. She enrolled in improv classes to learn how she could be authentically engaging in the moment. Equipped with new communication skills, Mary volunteered to perform a skit at the beginning of an all-hands meeting in her company. To the surprise and delight of her co-workers, Mary performed a parody of herself in the all-hands meeting. Her improv class paid off, as she brought the house down laughing and ending with thunderous applause.

Mary surprised everyone by doing something entirely out of her "pain in the ass" brand and extremely funny. She knew she needed to exhibit a radical behavioral change that would be amplified across the entire organization for all to see the *real* Mary. Instantly, her reputation was reframed. She then started every meeting with energizing humor. People began to look forward to working with her. People admired Mary's courage. She inspired rather than cut down others. Her push for excellence became a team goal, not her own personal crusade.

The mask had been shattered and the real Mary shone through. On her next 360 feedback report, the data revealed a 180-degree turnaround. People still tell the story of her skit. She contacted me several years later to let me know she had gotten a promotion, and her leadership ability to inspire continued improving.

Mary exemplified *Being the Real Deal* by her showing up, speaking up and taking courageous action to show others the real Mary. She knew who she was deep down in her roots. If people don't see the real you, your intentions and actions may be called into question. But if people see and are inspired by the real you, they will want you on their team. Organizations need to build cultures where sharing honest feedback in real-time is valued, expected, requested and welcome. In a culture of honesty, transparency and integrity, people say the truth to each other's faces, not behind their backs.

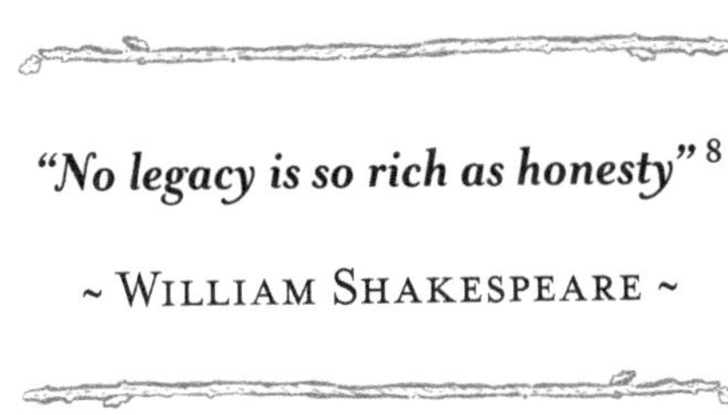

"No legacy is so rich as honesty" [8]

~ WILLIAM SHAKESPEARE ~

Integrity Is Not Optional

People can develop many leadership skills, but if the taproot of integrity is not firmly planted, temptations can topple even the mightiest. How do we strengthen our ability to withstand the storms of temptations we all face in our lives? Leaders must hold themselves to a higher standard than simply is it "legal." We must require leaders to be ethical, honest, factual, and transparent.

Sounds like lofty ideals—just be honest. Simple advice but challenging to do when the proverbial "shit hits the fan." Will your integrity keep you from getting fired? Will your integrity ensure the promotion you deserve? What if the organizational culture you are in does not want the truth?

In fact, the cost of honesty can be high in organizational cultures built on not telling the truth from the top down. These can be tough career-limiting decisions. Do you fight for change or find a place valuing the "unvarnished truth"? Lying is wrong, creates dysfunction in all relationships, and destroys a leader's credibility. An organizational culture built on telling people what they want to hear versus telling the truth is deadly.

"Integrity is number one. It did not make a difference what other skill sets the individual had. [. . .] Integrity is defined by your actions. Do people take situational shortcuts based on outcomes they want to achieve? Do actions match the rhetoric?" [9]

~ STEPHEN ZELNAK ~

Retired CEO & Chairman of Martin Marietta

Throughout history, people have always judged others based on the answer to one simple question: "Can I trust you?" The answer is either a yes or no. Even a "maybe" causes doubt, which leads to a no. Don't spend your time trying to discern the shades of gray when, in fact, it's just either you have integrity, or you don't. There is no such thing as "flexible morals."

If you don't keep your word, you may get the benefit of the doubt once, but people will always ask themselves: "Were you 'blowing smoke up my wazoo' to avoid the conflict? Did you know from the beginning you could never deliver on your commitment? Why did you not just level with me at the beginning? Overpromising and under-delivering have made me look like a fool in front of my customers and my peers. This is the last time I trust you."

Integrity is an absolute for all leaders. Leadership development programs have for years put in competencies, such as "Walking the talk, Tells the unvarnished truth, Is widely trusted" to measure the behaviors for integrity. These behaviors provide a reflection of what others experience as your integrity.

Who we are on the inside—our character—our values—having a taproot of integrity—is fundamental to *Being the Real Deal*. Yet we take integrity as a given and do not spend the time in self-reflection to learn about how who we are translates into our actions and decisions daily.

**"If you sacrifice your principles, there is no second chance.
If you miss your numbers, you get a second chance,
but you don't if you sacrifice your principles."** [10]

~ JAMES SINEGAL JR. ~
Retired co-founder and CEO of Costco

Integrity Is Needed to Grow Collaboration

We live in such a fast, speed-obsessed, big data, social media world where taking the time to understand yourself as a leader from the inside out seems like a luxury—or worse, a waste of time. Reflection doesn't appear to "move the ball forward," to be action-oriented and to be producing results—it's just soft and fluffy. The fact is, a *deep understanding of who you are from the inside out is the hardest, most important work you will ever do to develop yourself as a leader.*

Beyond getting to know yourself, few, if any, take the time up front when working with others to get to know the person behind the job title, role or Zoom screen. As one of my clients reminded me one day, "Vicky, you don't know what kinds of traumatic experiences other people are carrying around in their heads and hearts." At work, we are rewarded for achieving our individual objectives. What we often fail to understand is getting to know others and helping others know who we are expedites everyone's success and are the seeds for collaboration.

There are literally thousands of leadership books substantiating the importance of knowing others and building strong, trusting relationships. Yet I am still surprised when people fail to build relationships on who you are, not just what you do.

Not long ago, I was conducting in-person interviews to get individual feedback for a group of senior executives. These leaders had worked in offices with glass walls next to each other for over 20 years. Yet many of them said they did not know each other well enough to give meaningful feedback on their peers. I was astounded.

We are now more isolated than we could have ever imagined. Covid-19 sent everyone home at the start of 2020 except for "essential workers." Working from home, homeschooling and all living 24/7 in the same space took its toll. Zoom meetings all day with our fellow workers were difficult. Essential workers had it much worse because they risked exposure to the Covid-19 virus going to work every day. Hybrid work environments quickly became more the rule rather than the exception.

All leaders must share honest, accurate information based on facts. Building and maintaining trusting relationships in a virtual world is an absolute necessity for leaders from all walks of life. Visits with your doctor, connecting with your team members around the globe, your extended family members, or the neighbor two doors down are now done virtually as much as in person.

True connection requires planning deliberate efforts to build relationships in a virtual world. Creating a sustained feeling of community requires honest, open dialogue in a safe and trusting environment. Collaboration requires building trusting relationships. Trust is required for genuine collaborative relationships. Honesty is required to have trust in any relationship.

Living One's Integrity—the Challenge

There was not a dry eye in the church sanctuary as the service continued. A tall, broad-shouldered, middle-aged man stepped up to the podium and began speaking, "Nancy knew where she came from, and she knew where she was going." Years later, I still remember these exact words starting Nancy's eulogy.

Nancy was one of the female pioneers in the Chicago business community. She had quickly moved up the ranks from first-line officer to group executive at a major Chicago bank. While I was still a professor, this same bank became my first organizational development consulting client in Chicago. An amazing group of director-level women leaders at the bank welcomed me as an external partner.

In a move that stunned the bank's senior leadership, Nancy chose to leave the bank after a 20-year distinguished career, rather than sacrifice her values. She explained why in a *Chicago Tribune* article: "I had gone as far as I could go," she said. "Women are not in top management at banks. I couldn't make that last rung, the boys wouldn't let me in—so I did it myself."[11]

Hitting the glass ceiling did not stop Nancy. She and a business partner started their own consulting firm. Both Nancy and her partner were role models and mentors to me and many other female entrepreneurs. When tested, Nancy acted with integrity and courage. Her actions demonstrated her integrity, her truth-telling to the world explained the injustice. She did not just leave, Nancy called out the inequality—she spoke truth to power publicly.

Experiencing an impenetrable glass ceiling myself, Nancy's successfully making the public leap to start her own business gave me confidence when starting my business. Having role models and mentors who are always *Being the Real Deal* inspired so many women like myself to believe in their power to be successful in their own businesses with integrity in the late 1980s and beyond.

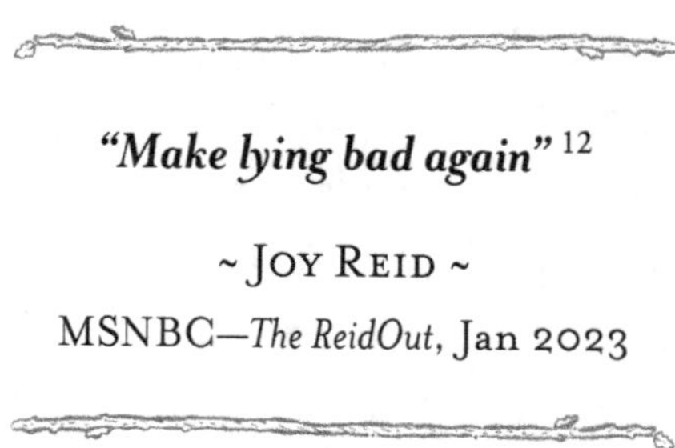

"Make lying bad again" [12]

~ JOY REID ~
MSNBC—*The ReidOut*, Jan 2023

When did we start calling lies disinformation? When did lies become alternative facts? Isn't disinformation simply lies? I agree passionately with the headline on a recent Joy Reid's MSNBC nightly news broadcast. We must make lies and lying bad again. Leaders who lie are hurting not only America, but the entire globe.

America's Integrity Crisis

Americans and people around the globe pay the price. This is not a typo mistake—these are life-and-death leadership failures. My experience coaching leaders from all walks of life has taught me that leaders without the taproot of integrity are not coachable. Integrity is basic to *Being the Real Deal* as a leader—"you either have it or you don't." People without integrity should not be in any leadership positions—not even top dogcatchers!

Integrity must be an absolute minimum criterion for any leadership position. Here is where learning what is on a person's invisible resume is so important when selecting a person for a leadership position. Is the person honest? Does the person tell the truth and insist on the truth from others? Is the person widely trusted? Do people view the person as *Being the Real Deal?*

"Integrity is an all-or-nothing virtue (like being half pregnant, there's no such thing as semi-integrity)." [13]

~ MARSHALL GOLDSMITH ~

Triggers: Sparking positive change and making it last

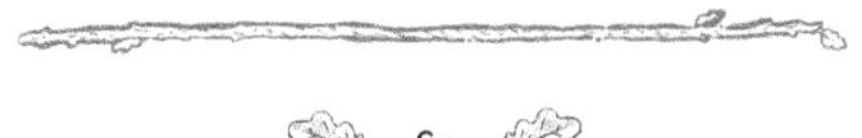

"The Big Lie" [14]

January 6th, 2021, a riotous mob attacked the Capitol of the United States of America with the explicit intention to overthrow the democratic process of a free and fair election—the bedrock of American democracy. Americans and the world watched as the unthinkable happened in real time.

Shocked, saddened, and fearful for people's lives, I watched the attack unfold, literally crying out at the television, "Where the hell are the forces to keep the Capitol and the Joint Session of Congress safe?" America's elected officials were in the process of their solemn constitutional duty of counting and certifying the electoral will of the American people. How could this attack on our democracy have happened?

"The Big Lie" [15] that the 2020 Presidential election had been stolen was spread and believed by many. The facts are the 2020 Presidential election was the fairest and most secure election in modern history, certified by all states and upheld by the courts—even the Supreme Court. [16] The peaceful transfer of power is essential to democracy.

As I worked on the final edits for this book, I could not leave out the attack on American democracy and "The Big Lie." People in powerful positions lied, and other powerful people supported the lies by repeating the lies. Had the efforts to overturn the 2020 U.S. election been successful, Americans would have lost the right to have their votes counted accurately and fairly. Criminal investigations, prosecutions and convictions continue. We will get to the entire truth about this attack on American democracy. As leadership coaches, leadership scholars, and leaders, we must call out lies and hold all leaders to the highest standards of integrity. We must "make lying bad again."[17] regardless of being in a powerful position or political views.

"There is truth and there are lies. Lies told for power and for profit. And each of us has a duty and responsibility, as citizens, as Americans and especially as leaders—leaders who have pledged to honor our Constitution and protect our nation—to defend the truth and to defeat the lies." [18]

~ JOSEPH R. BIDEN ~

46th President of the United States of America

Inaugural Address, January 20, 2021

Keep Growing!

Do you consistently:

1. **Tell the truth—to yourself and others**
   ~ Are you honest even when it is not in your best interests?

2. **Act in accordance with the truth**
   ~ Do your deeds match words?

3. **Take responsibility**
   ~ Are you accountable and do you speak truth to power?

4. **Prioritize the needs of others**
   ~ Do you put employees, shareholders, and the community above your own personal gain?

5. **Act altruistically**
   ~ Do you actively make the world a better place for all?

"For there is always light.
If only we're brave enough to see it.
If only we're brave enough to be it." [19]

~ Amanda Gorman ~
"The Hill We Climb"

CHAPTER FOUR

The Heart of the Matter

*"Heartwood is the central supporting pillar
of the tree . . . as strong as steel."* [1]

~ Gretchen C. Daily and Charles J. Katz Jr. ~

The Power of Trees

Passionate Purpose—Your Why—Is the Heartwood of Inspiring Leadership

What do you love about your work? I always ask leaders this question when discussing the possibility of our working together. Why ask about "loving the work"? A leader needs her own personal "fire in the belly." Your heart's desire to "Aspire Higher."[2] Your red-hot passionate purpose is your "heartwood—stronger than steel." Your heartfelt why—your purpose fuels positive energy and inspires others to commit to the work of a shared purpose.

My experience has taught me, *leaders who embody a passionate purpose do so from a place of love.* No matter the type of work, loving what you do and loving the people you work with is essential. If you passionately love your work and know what you do makes a real difference, then and only then are you inspired by the heart of the matter.

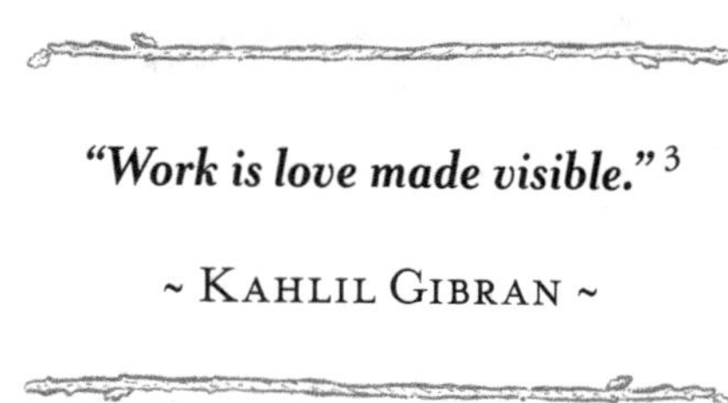

"Work is love made visible." [3]

~ KAHLIL GIBRAN ~

Leaders who are passionate about their purpose ignite passion in others for their purpose. Others literally feel the love you genuinely have for the work and for the people you are leading. As the iconic tennis champion Billie Jean King advised, "Your head needs to be in the game, your heart needs to be in the game and your guts need to be in the game."[4]

Athletes and coaches know; musicians and symphony conductors know; soldiers and their generals know; surgeons and their operating teams know; sales leaders and their salespeople know; and teachers and their students know. They all know "loving the work" is inspiring. Doesn't matter the field, the job, the company or the country, leading from a place of loving the work and loving the people doing the work inspires others.

Meraki μεράκι (Greek)
"To do something with soul, creativity, or love; to leave a piece of essence of yourself in your work" [5]

The Greek word Meraki (may-rah-kee) does not have a word-for-word translation in English. However, the expression ". . . describes how a person loves what they do in life, and they display effort, care and interest in what they are doing."[6] We have known from the ancient Greeks to today's analysis of the Great Resignation of 2021–2022 that purpose creates passion for our work lives. We know work's rewards are more than pay.

Having done many employee climate/engagement/culture surveys for organizations, the response to one question always speaks volumes about people's connection to an organization's purpose. The question: "Does what I do in my job make a difference in the company's success?" In other words, do I make a difference in achieving the company's purpose? We may be vastly different as individuals, but when it comes to basic needs, we are all human. We need to feel connected and valued both for who we are and what we do. Can we feel loved, appreciated and respected as part of our work experience? Nothing less will create an inspired and inspiring work culture.

In research published in January 2022 in the *MIT Sloan Management Review*, Sull, Sull, and Zweig[7] found:

1. "Toxic Culture Is Driving the Great Resignation."

2. The Great Resignation was ". . . affecting blue-collar and white-collar sectors with equal force."

3. Pay concerns were listed at 16th on the list of concerns predicting employee turnover.

4. "A toxic corporate culture, for example, is 10.4 times more powerful than compensation in predicting a company's attribution rate compared with its industry."

5. ". . . leading elements contributing to toxic cultures include failure to promote diversity, equity, and inclusion; workers feeling disrespected; and unethical behavior."

We know a great deal about toxic work cultures; however, it is time for leaders to do better than just not create a toxic culture. Leaders are responsible for planting and cultivating an inspiring culture. Employee engagement is more than words on a mission and values statement. Humans have always hungered for meaningful work that brings them joy. People who love their work, love the people they work with and know they make a difference—feel valued.

"I've learned that people will forget what you said, people will forget what you did, but people will never forget how you made them feel." [8]

~ DR. MAYA ANGELOU ~

Loving the Why, What, How and Who of the Work

Flashback to the fall of 1985 with me. I departed from the consulting firm which had recruited me from academia. As part of the happy divorce from the firm, I retained a major client project I had contracted. With no business cards, no business plan and no impressive corporate office, I launched my own organizational development consulting and leadership coaching firm.

Sitting at my makeshift desk in the unfinished basement of our first small house on the northwest side of Chicago, I did not have the typical trappings of business or academic success. What I did have was a burning passion to do "big league" organizational development consulting based on my strongly held values of integrity, courage, and humility.

Helping individuals, teams and organizations grow and develop is the work I love. Helping leaders to succeed at making major improvements in their leadership effectiveness is my mission. Demonstrating I could be successful in business while at the same time holding true to my values meant creating a business not about billable hours, but about delivering transformational improvements.

My love and passion for helping my clients improve is not just about business—it's deeply personal. Twenty years later, the CFO of a multibillion-dollar international corporation said to me at our initial meeting, "You are different. You will walk away from the business opportunity if it's not the right thing for the client—it's more than business to you."

I thanked the CFO for the feedback. Clearly, she "got me" and the why, what, how and who of our organizational development and coaching process. I was not "selling" my services. I was asking for a real commitment for leadership behavioral improvement on her part. If there was any chance of her team improving, the CFO's leadership behaviors had to improve first.

Creating improvements that make a real difference in people's lives and doing it with integrity, respect and, yes, fun is what keeps "a skip in my step." My view has always been making money is an outcome of always doing the right thing for the client, customers, employees and community.

"I would like to be known as an intelligent woman, a courageous woman, a loving woman, a woman who teaches by being." [9]

~ DR. MAYA ANGELOU ~

Loving the Work

Telling people about my values-based organizational and leadership development consulting firm sounded vague and theoretical. Potential clients needed to experience working with me to see my values in action. So, my marketing strategy was to give free speeches at luncheon and dinner meetings to professional groups made up of potential clients. I had no money for a "formal marketing campaign," and the internet was still being invented.

Getting in front of a room full of potential clients at professional meetings and having them experience what my organizational development consulting could do for them proved to be excellent marketing. Interestingly, no matter the group meeting, the meal always came with cold green beans. I referred to this marketing strategy as working the "green bean circuit."

The speeches focused on leadership, teamwork and transformational change. The presentations were interactive, high-energy, engaging, fun, as well as educational. After almost every presentation, several people from the audience would come up, say their team or company could use my help, and ask for my business card.

I spoke to professional associations of every kind from accountants, nurses, engineers, hospital CEOs, to telecommunications union members to door salespersons. Yes, there is a professional association for people who sell doors!

After a cocktail hour and dinner, I had my work cut out for me, so I would pull out all the stops. I would engage the attendees in team-building exercises after their meal, which of course included—you guessed it—cold green beans. From exercises with balloons to my *Oprah* impersonation interviewing audience members, these engaging activities usually left the audience wanting more.

After one evening presentation to a statewide plants and ground association, a person rushed to the front of the room, grabbed my hand, and started vigorously shaking it. "I really need your help to build teamwork. Would you consider working with us?" he asked. I automatically said yes, thinking to myself, *Thank you God! I may have landed a new client.*

We exchanged business cards and agreed I would call him the next morning to discuss the details of our working together. Looking down at the card, I saw he was Head of Facilities Management at a large suburban high school.

The next morning at 8:30 a.m. sharp, I phoned my potential new client. "First, I need background on the team and their situation. Then I will develop a specific process to help your team improve working together," I said.

He began: "I have a group of janitors in my school I cannot get to work together."

Honestly, I was surprised the client was a group of janitors. Why surprised? First, I had assumed the team members would have managerial roles. Secondly, rarely did frontline employees in facilities management get this kind of investment to build teamwork.

Typically, if things are not working, janitorial employees are fired and replaced. As we continued talking, I heard genuine caring in his voice. He shared his frustration, "Individually, these are wonderful people; but for some reason, nothing we have done has improved the situation." This leader was stuck and was convinced I could help. Partnering with him and his group of warring janitors was my next client project.

This was not exactly what I had prepared myself to do in my Ph. D. studies. My dissertation research was a study of senior executives' leadership behaviors in the banking industry implementing large-scale technical innovation. However, engaging people in the process of identifying the root causes of problems and having them commit to improvements is the same, whether they're senior executives or frontline employees. This group of janitors turned out to be amazing teachers for me. Working with them was an inspiring learning experience that taught me lifelong lessons I continue to apply to all leaders' development efforts.

"Mud When It Rains"

Gathering data on the situation from everyone was an important first step to engaging individuals. I designed a questionnaire for the janitors to answer individually to identify the group's problems. One of the questions I asked was, "What's the most difficult part of your job?" As I read the answers, I began putting the puzzle together of why there was no teamwork.

Then, I read an answer to one of the questions on the questionnaire which I will never forget. The question: "What is the hardest part of your job?" The answer: "Mud when it rains." At first, I thought maybe the person was trying to be funny, but then as I read further, I realized the person was dead serious. I thought to myself, "What can I do to help this person with mud when it rains?'" My answer was: "Absolutely nothing." There is always going to be "mud when it rains." In the job of janitor, you just must deal with mud as best as you can.

No matter what your job is, whether CEO or night-shift nurse supervisor, there is always some kind of "mud when it rains." There are parts of every job that cannot be changed. It is simply the nature of work. Dealing with "mud when it rains" can be a passion killer if it is not connected to your values and purpose.

Sometimes it's not the job, but the organization's dysfunctional culture. When I was a full-time professor, one of the academic departments I worked in was unable to recognize the need for growth. They were on the decade model of change. "We'll get it done this decade or the next." Although I loved teaching and conducting research, my "mud when it rains" was more like being in a mud pit up to my neck in inertia. My need to grow new programs, innovate, create and drive systemic change was just not going to happen in this department. So, I left academia for a career in organizational development consulting and leadership coaching where transformational change is the name of the game.

The question now becomes, what is "mud when it rains" for you? What are the things you cannot change? If there are things that are not going to change and are not meeting your passion-driven purpose—what will? Complaining about "mud when it rains" wastes precious energy needed to keep the "skip in your step" as a leader. Let me be clear, working to transform the "mud" into fertile ground can be a worthwhile effort.

Focus your attention, time and efforts on improving what you can. And remember, no matter what job, career, company, there is always going to be some kind of "mud when it rains." Do not let it dampen your spirits. Instead, remind yourself of the "fire in your belly" for your passion-driven purpose. Mud and rain are needed to grow the seeds of improvement you are planting. Transformational change is messy. Be honest and candid about the struggle, as well as the victory—both are important parts of an inspiring leadership journey. Find the joy in the journey for yourself and your team.

"Some people feel the rain. Others just get wet." [10]

~ BOB MARLEY ~

Collaboration: The Key to Achieving Your Heartfelt Purpose

After analyzing the janitors' needs assessment data, there were difficult aspects to the janitors' jobs. However, the janitors loved working at the school and loved the students. Each person was trying to individually achieve his or her own job—to keep a specific area of the school clean.

The needs assessment also painted a clear picture of a group at war with each other. I knew the team development work with them had to unearth and resolve their conflict. As we discussed their needs assessment answers, it became clear all were hardworking and did whatever it took to do their individual job. A core issue was the team leader's total focus on individual performance and one-on-one feedback.

Because of all the focus on one's individual job and not on keeping the entire school clean and sanitary, a rather dysfunctional behavioral pattern had developed. The janitors were stealing each other's mops (literally). People constantly had to hunt down their mops to clean their area, wasting time and generating anger and distrust.

Every time I listen to senior executives complain about "silos" and the inability to share resources across functions, I have this flashback to my mop-stealing group of janitors. Honestly, how many of us have failed to share people, budgets or other resources for fear of being caught short-staffed? If you are only accountable for your area, what happens to others becomes their problem and not yours.

Today, collaboration is required for individual, team and organizational success. Yet organizations still struggle for all to "play nice," "share the ball" or "take one for the team." Regrettably, a siloed mentality is still prevalent in many work cultures. Global organizations face intense collaboration challenges of times zones, cultural norms, virtual teams and communication barriers.

For the janitors to stop stealing each other's mops, a purpose greater than getting their individual work accomplished had to be collectively developed. The team's purpose had to be more important than cleaning a single bathroom or hallway. The team's purpose had to inspire collaboration.

We discussed what would happen if parts of the school were not clean. Then it dawned on everyone: They realized that unless all of them were successful, the health department could close the school. The look of pride on their faces lit up the room when they realized how important their work was to the students and to the school they loved.

Without their collective work, the school could be shut down by the state's health department. As for stealing mops, they realized this behavior caused distrust. All agreed the mop-stealing behavior had to stop immediately. They figured out they had to start sharing resources and help each other.

What did working with this group of janitors teach me? First, no matter what your job—whether it is cleaning a bathroom, making a sale, or preparing a departmental budget—people need to feel the work they are doing makes a difference. Their work must be valued first by themselves and second by the entire organization. Knowing in your heart you are making a difference creates energy, passion and pride. There is a "skip in your step" even as you deal with your "mud when it rains."

Stealing each other's mops is a short-term fix for a systemic problem—the lack of collaboration among individuals. We don't live in a world anymore where just doing your job will lead to the team's or organization's success. We live in a world where collaboration is the key ingredient to individual, team and organizational success.

Remember, actions have unintended consequences. We're often blind to others' perceptions of our actions and our perceived intentions. Taking someone else's mop when you need it might seem like a logical, non-controversial thing to do in the moment. Yet to the person whose mop has been taken, you are considered a thief, and the unresolved conflict dance begins.

I saw, throughout the course of our work together, individuals who started out at war with each other literally turn into a team with new ways of sharing resources. I saw a group of people see and feel the difference their work made to the students and school they all genuinely loved. They began walking a little taller throughout their workday. It was more important to ensure the entire school was clean than just their individual part. Working together was satisfying, fun and energizing.

These individuals becoming a real team inspired me. Engaging people so they get fired up to achieve their passion-driven purpose feels magical. In our work together, we unearthed the roots of distrust and planted new seeds of understanding. We had started growing real-time cooperation. I saw people step up and change to make things better. When people feel deep in their bones that what they are doing each day makes a difference, then real engagement happens. We all desire for our work to be valued. People who feel valued show up, step up and can create real improvements.

Leading With Inspiration and Passion

When I interviewed William Green, who at the time was President and CEO of Accenture, he said that one of the essential qualities that CEOs must have is the "ability to inspire. . . ."[11] A defining difference among leaders is their ability to inspire passion for a purpose. Inspiring others first starts within you as a leader. If you are not feeling the "fire in the belly," fake energy and enthusiasm quickly flame out. If you cannot find passion within yourself, then it is almost impossible for you as a leader to genuinely elicit passion in others.

"Great leaders elicit passion, not perfection . . . to bring people past the limitations of their own potential is leadership." [12]

~ LORIN MAAZEL ~
New York Philharmonic Music Director (2002–2009)

We all feel the magical energy of passion when it is present. When passion isn't present, we also feel the dull emptiness of pointless effort. Eliciting passion does not come from our abilities as analytical, technical experts. As Martha Graham, renowned dancer and dance teacher explained, "Great dancers are not great because of their technique—they are great because of their passion."[13]

To elicit passion, you must own the purpose—for the love of *what* are you pursuing the purpose? When I interviewed Githesh Ramamurthy, Chairman and CEO of CCCIS, and asked him to describe a leader who is The Real Deal, he answered, "It is first and foremost about passion, because you cannot fake it. It is either there or it is not there. A test for that passion is, if you were not getting paid for it, would you still do it? If you think of your organization as volunteers, would they still do the work if they were not paid? That means they are motivated by a higher cause—a greater reason."[14]

"To play a wrong note is insignificant; to play without passion is inexcusable." [15]

~ LUDWIG VAN BEETHOVEN ~

Owning the Purpose

One of the many blessings in my career was being selected to work as an external leadership coach for Dell in 2000. Michael Dell, Founder and Chairman, and his senior team had set the example of getting 360 feedback and crafting a leadership development plan using external coaches. This was an innovative leadership and talent development process at the time. Dell's senior leadership found the feedback and coaching such a powerful development process that all of Dell's people managers were to participate in a 360-leadership development process and work with an external coach. This was a massive undertaking by the leaders of the organizational and talent development team.

Dell had been on fire with growth. Hiring the best and the brightest was essential. Dell's early employees of all types and levels received stock ownership in the company. I quickly learned the employee number on your employee badge was important. Individuals would introduce themselves to me, "I am employee number 56" and beam with great pride. A low number gave you bragging rights. It meant you had been at Dell from the beginning and had worked directly with "Michael." It also meant you were still at Dell because you wanted to be at Dell, not because you needed the job. These first employees were, in fact, "volunteers."

What was surprising to Dell newcomers was the fact these first employees were some of the most committed and passionate. They were die-hard keepers of Dell's start-up culture. They financially did not need the job; they were working because they loved their work and loved Dell. They owned Dell's success.

Even as the company grew, volunteers continued the infamous tradition of having brown-bag lunches with Michael, where everyone including Michel brought their own lunch—in a brown bag. This is a tradition started in the company's early days, where all had a say at the table to talk about what was happening in the business and give "unvarnished" feedback on all things Dell.

I coached over 100 leaders through Dell's 360 leadership development process. These were bright, aggressive and hungry learners who desperately wanted to excel in their leadership roles at Dell. "Volunteers" were especially fun to coach because of their great stories of what it was like at the beginning and their continued "fire in the belly" passion for the company. The entrepreneurial spirit and drive for results were at the heart of Dell's culture.

The wave of growth was like a tsunami that never ended but just picked up more and more speed. Few had ever experienced this, so new employees—fondly called "newbies"—were easily identified by the "deer in the headlights look on their faces." For at least the first 3 months, and often longer, "newbies" struggled with the speed, volume, and what to say yes to and what to say no to as demands far exceeded 24 hours in the day. Most learned how to navigate the growth storm.

Even though leaders gave realistic previews of the job demands and culture to candidates, until you were in it, the speed, the pace of change and the sheer magnitude of work was unimaginable. One year working at Dell was considered equal to 5 years at another company. People talked about how long they had worked at the company in "Dell years."

People were excited, challenged and filled with passion to win in the marketplace. Working at Dell meant you owned the company's success. Yes, they did also have miniature car races down the aisles of office cubicles. The energy was infectious and could be felt when you walked into different buildings.

I still stay in touch with leaders I worked with during this time. Some still work at Dell and others have climbed their career ladders elsewhere. During my time coaching at Dell, there was a kind of magic in the air. There was this common sense among employees, leaders, coaches and vendors alike that we all owned Dell's success and we all made a difference.

What I learned as a leadership coach at Dell was worth 5 years of coaching at other places. Leaders elicit passion and inspire others by having them own the company's success—not leader-owned.

Gail McGovern, President & CEO of the American Red Cross, advises, "Nonprofits don't have a monopoly on meaning. At Fidelity Investments, we didn't just manage money—we helped people fulfill their dreams for college or retirement. Your job as a leader is to tap into the power of that higher purpose—and you can't do it by retreating to the analytical. If you want to lead, have the courage to do it from the heart."[16]

Leading From the Heart

"Leaders touch a heart before they ask for a hand." [17]

~ JOHN C. MAXWELL ~

People all over the world need to collaborate from a place of love for each other in real time. The global Covid-19 pandemic has demonstrated the need for collaboration in the deadliest way. We must care for each other in all situations. Leaders must unite to take collective, caring actions to keep each other safe and be prepared for the next deadly global pandemic and other challenges. We must care for the health and safety of all people. This higher purpose is now a clarion call to unite in support of our common humanity.

When faced with another difficult health challenge a few years ago, I asked my therapist shaman Doris, "How am I going to get through this one?" She answered, "We are going to love our way through this."

Leaders in all organizations and all governments throughout the world must find ways for us to love our way through the multitude of crises happening simultaneously. The global climate crisis, Covid-19 pandemic, and now another unthinkable crisis—a land war in Europe—tests our love for our fellow humans. Russia's unprovoked invasion of its neighbor Ukraine has created one of the greatest humanitarian crisis since World War 2. As the war rages on, we face the real possibility of World War 3.

We are witnessing a global example of the strength of a higher purpose creating a steel resolve where the cost is life or death. Ukrainians are not only fighting for their homes and homeland, but they are also risking everything for freedom and democracy.

Prime Minster Zelensky explains that "we saw slaves shooting at free people, slaves of propaganda that replaced their conscience." He adds that the war has turned ordinary Ukrainians into heroes and "the enemy doesn't believe it's all real . . . There is no need to organize resistance," Zelensky adds. "Resistance for Ukrainians is part of their soul."[18]

The courage of the Ukrainian people embodied in their leader Prime Minster Zelensky is inspiring the free world to help fight against authoritarian unprovoked aggression. To inspire our life's work, we need to passionately believe in a purpose worthy of the best in us for all of us. Leading from the heart with integrity and courage, "we shall overcome"[19] even the toughest of global challenges. Our higher passionate purpose must be driven by our love for our leadership work and our love of our fellow humans.

Keep Growing!

1. What do you love about your work?

2. What do you love about the people you work with and the people you serve?

3. How is "Meraki" evident in your leadership behaviors?

4. How are you dealing (in a positive way) with your "mud when it rains"?

5. What can you do to inspire a more passionate commitment to your higher purpose in yourself and others?

"Leadership is about empathy. It is about having the ability to relate to and connect with people for the purpose of inspiring and empowering their lives." [20]

~ OPRAH WINFREY ~

CHAPTER FIVE

Paying the Price

"*I can see in the acorn the oak tree. I see the growth,
the rebuilding, the restoring. I see that is the American psyche.
There is so much we can draw understanding from. One of the
lessons is the development of courage. Because without courage,
you can't practice any of the other virtues consistently.*"[1]

~ DR. MAYA ANGELOU ~

Leadership Courage Can Grow

A sign in one of my favorite neighborhood breakfast places reads, "What if the Hokey Pokey is what it's all about?" Every time I see the sign, I laugh out loud. Do you know this childhood dance—the Hokey Pokey? When my elementary school teacher put on the Hokey Pokey record, we'd all jump out of our desk chairs and start following the dance instructions which ended with:

> *"You put your whole self in, you take your whole self out, you put your whole self in, and you shake it all about, you do the hokey pokey and turn yourself around. That's what it's all about!"*[2]

Seriously, putting your whole self in, showing up with integrity, and stepping up with courage to speak truth to power, *IS* what it's all about as a leader. What does it take to put your whole self in when others are painfully silent? Courage. When tested, we dig deep, call up our heart's passionate purpose and act with honesty despite the fear. We find courage rooted in our integrity. Courage to call out wrongdoing. Courage to advocate for a better way forward. Courage to tell the truth even when others flee in fear from the bright lights of facts.

According to Githesh Ramamurthy, Chairman and CEO of CCCIS, leaders who are the Real Deal have three key behaviors separating them from leaders who are Not the Real Deal.

> *"Behavior number one is the willingness to pay the price for the principle. You follow through with your actions knowing there is a price to pay.*

The second behavior is the leader has the same behavior in public as in private.

The third behavior is the person demonstrates principles through their actions not just through their words. Their behaviors are a model derived from deeper principles."[3]

Taking risks and accepting the consequences of living values of integrity, compassion, respect and humility requires courage. Chairman and CEO Githesh Ramamurthy leads with absolute integrity, humility and principled behavior—yes, he is absolutely the Real Deal!

Chairman Ramamurthy is a brilliant technologist and successful global business leader who, to my knowledge, never sacrifices his deeply held principles. Githesh inspires great loyalty and deep commitment because he lives his principles and is willing to "pay the price" while displaying quiet courage and humility. One of the true joys and honors of my career has been my work with Githesh and his team.

Physical Courage

We all clearly recognize physical courage. We celebrate those who in times of crisis exhibit the highest levels of bravery imaginable. They heroically face the ultimate risk: saving others' lives while risking their own lives. Hearing their amazing stories, we are rightly in awe of these brave souls. We ask ourselves, "Could I ever be that brave?"

In 2020, the bravest among us were frontline, essential workers. These women and men went to work every day knowing they could be exposed to the deadly Covid-19 virus, be infected, and die. On top of this life-or-death risk was the ever-present reality that they could unknowingly take the deadly virus home to their loved ones.

Yet, these courageous individuals persisted. Showing up daily to check out groceries, clean hospitals, drive buses and comfort dying Covid-19 patients on ventilators as their last breaths were taken without any loved ones near. Physical courage was redefined by nurses, respiratory therapists, ER doctors, hospital sanitation crews, police, firefighters, EMTs, bus drivers, grocery clerks, all types of jobs essential for all of us to survive during the worst global public health crisis in over 100 years.

They exhibited daily courage as these essential workers witnessed some of their fellow workers contract the deadly virus and make the ultimate sacrifice. Remarkable, brave individuals, from teachers to healthcare workers to so many unsung heroes, faced fear every day as they masked up to do their jobs in a worldwide health crisis of epic proportions.

"Courage is not the absence of fear. Courage is fear walking." [4]

~ SUSAN DAVID, PH. D. ~

Moral Courage

There are many acts of courage we all exhibit when faced with everyday situations calling for us to live our values regardless of the personal consequences. It's those daily moments of truth where *Being the Real Deal* requires courage. Some days we are required to be more courageous than others. Some acts of courage go unnoticed. Some acts of courage, like Rosa Parks refusing to go to the back of the bus and "paying the price" fuel the way forward in our fight for social justice and equality.

A leader's lack of courage—cowardice in the face of personal risk, failure to act with integrity—has become all too commonplace. Sadly, too many leaders have become comfortable with not telling the truth and have gotten by with spreading false information. Lies have been weaponized to weaken democracies around the world. Facts based on hard evidence are no longer accepted as accurate by far too many.

Embodying Moral Courage and Physical Courage in the Fight for Freedom

February 2022 brought the world another unthinkable crisis—a land war in Europe. Russia launched an unprovoked invasion of Ukraine. Slaughter of innocent civilians and multiple war crimes have been documented. The war wages on, as of this moment, as heroic Ukrainians led by a young President defy the odds—a true David and Goliath[5] matchup.

The moral and physical courage exemplified by Ukrainian President Zelensky is inspiring the world to fight for democracy and freedom against the murderous dictatorship exemplified by Russia's President Putin. As Kyiv was being violently attacked, the President and his family chose to stay in Kyiv and lead by example. President Zelensky is reported to have said when offered safe passage out of Kyiv, "The fight is here, I need ammunition not a ride."[6]

Being Tested

Do you put your whole self in when you lead? Not every day requires us to "leave it all on the field." But those times when we are tested, when our roots are shaken require courage. It's those not-so-obvious tests that show us and others who we really are.

We get tested all the time with all kinds of consequences. For the vast majority of us, it is not the big legal-illegal questions that test us. It doesn't take courage to say, "Let's stay out of jail." It is the micro-moments in our daily lives that never make the headlines that require us to pay a price to stand strong in our principles. Because of our taproot of integrity, we can withstand the strong winds of temptation. We may be bowed by life's storms, but never broken or uprooted.

These no-brainer decisions are high reward and low risk, or vice versa, low reward and high risk. The decisions that do test us are the ones that are high risk and high reward. Decisions that have competing and conflicting interests are those requiring courage to stay true to our values despite pressures to do otherwise.

In a difficult situation, do you see risk as an opportunity, or do you freeze with fear? How do you make the tough call? How do you stand in your heartfelt knowledge of what is right, honest, and ethical, especially at work?

The ability to "meet the moment" as a leader requires the courage to override our feeling of vulnerability. Inspiring leaders act bravely despite their fear. Our bravery is a matter of practice. Small acts of courage based on our strongly held values build a reservoir of courage when faced with challenges requiring even greater acts of bravery.

Can you think of times you have chosen the harder path because it was the right thing? Our moments of truth come in small and large opportunities and challenges. Some decisions though seemingly small and insignificant are growing our roots of courage that spread deep and wide, supporting us throughout a lifetime.

"At the heart of daring leadership is a deeply human truth that is rarely acknowledged, especially at work: Courage and fear are not mutually exclusive. Most of us feel brave and afraid at the exact same time. We feel vulnerable." [7]

~ BRENÉ BROWN, PH. D, LMSW ~

Learning to Be Courageous

We learn to overcome our fears and act with courage from our earliest days. One of my favorite stories of courage and vulnerability was shared with me by my amazing Aunt Wilma James Gordon, a lifelong early childhood teacher.

My Aunt Wilma ran a preschool in the Blue Ridge Mountains of North Carolina. At the end of every school year, her 25 preschoolers presented a program for parents where the children all sing as a group.

As the little ones began singing their first song one year, my Aunt Wilma noticed that Josh, in the front row, was not singing. He just stood straight as an arrow. They sang another song and Josh did not open his mouth. He looked like he was frozen in place. The final song came, and once again Josh just stood next to his friends, still not singing. As the applause rang out from the parents, my Aunt Wilma worried about what she would say to Josh the next morning about his performance.

The next day Josh ran into the classroom, straight to my Aunt Wilma's desk. He blurted out, "Aren't you proud of me, Miss Wilma? It was all I could do to stand there with everyone and not run back to my mama."

Aunt Wilma smiled and said, "Yes, Josh, I am very proud of you because you didn't run back to your mama. You stood with the other children for all three songs!" She gave him a big hug for his courage. Josh ran back to his desk beaming with pride for his brave accomplishment. Maybe, just maybe next time Josh will be leading the singing.[8]

"The more slowly trees grow at the first, the sounder they are at the core, and I think the same is true of human beings." [9]

~ HENRY DAVID THOREAU ~

My "Listen Sweetie" Moment of Truth

The second year of my business presented me with one of the most important moments of truth for who I am as a professional. My defining moment wasn't based on a business strategy, but it certainly became one. This decision set me on a path enabling me for the rest of my career to work with amazing integrity-driven leaders and their organizations. The "moment of truth" was at the root of my values and my ability to be an ethical consultant and coach.

Briefcase in hand, dressed in my red power suit, I was ready to be the best consultant this bank President could ever consider for improving customer service. Yes, I had all the trappings of expertise required to get the consulting contract. I looked confident on the outside. However, what could not be seen was the *"Oh my God, I need to land a new client"* knot that was ever-present in my stomach as an entrepreneur. When will I ever stop stressing about finding new clients? Answer: Never. Putting yourself in situations for acceptance or rejection daily as an entrepreneur is walking with vulnerability.

Having gotten lost twice trying to find the bank building, I stepped quickly to the security desk. "Hi, I'm Dr. Gordon, I am here for a 2:00 p.m. appointment with Mr. um . . . the President." Damn, I had blanked on his name—it was 1:59 p.m. As I was ushered into the President's office, the knot tightened in my stomach and reminded me of how much I needed a new client. This was the only "hot prospect" I had. I gave the President my best smile and a strong but not knuckle-breaking handshake. We went into his office.

The President was a man in his early fifties. The office and the man looked like "The President of the Bank" right down to his gold cuff links and pictures of him golfing with the President of the United States on the credenza behind his mammoth mahogany desk.

As with every potential client, you must pass the "do we connect?" chemistry test. We did the "get to know you" game. We connected, thanks to his customer's recommendation of me, who was also his great friend and golfing buddy.

After passing the connection test, I asked him: "What are your biggest customer service challenges?" I continued interviewing him to identify the bank's needs and determine successful outcomes for the customer service improvement effort.

As he answered the questions, I suddenly realized he was referring to me as "sweetie." At first, I thought he must have forgotten my name. So, I inserted my name and references to myself as Vicky as I continued gathering information on the bank's customer service needs. He continued to refer to me as "sweetie."

"SWEETIE"—like a bucket of cold water thrown directly into my face. What the hell was he thinking? First, I thought, give him the benefit of the doubt. But then my moment of truth arrived. I leaned forward, stared directly into his eyes, paused for emphasis, then asked: "What are your leadership behaviors you think might need to change to support and help create improved customer service?"

Dead silence. Then leaning across his mammoth mahogany desk, the President said, "Listen sweetie, I am not the problem. You need to focus these efforts on the staff and the tellers." *What?* He was clueless. I continued the interview as if nothing had happened.

My mind was racing. Could I expect him to change? The lack of respect for how he talked to me was clearly how he talked to the tellers and staff. He refused to be a part of the effort, no matter how I positioned it with him. This was not for him; it was for his tellers and staff. He did not need any improvement. The bank's tellers and staff were the problem.

To my astonishment, he asked me for a proposal. It was crystal clear to me nothing I could do would work without his participation and partnership. This was my test: I needed the business. However, if I took the project, I would be taking the bank's money knowing whatever I did would not work. The effort would be a failure. I had jumped through all the hoops to get the President to ask me for a proposal and say he wanted to work with me. I sat silent for what felt like an eternity.

Knowing the truth about the situation, would I go against my strongly held principle to deliver real improvement outcomes for clients, not just activities? The knot in my stomach got tighter.

Finally, I said, "Thank you for your time and this opportunity. However, I am not the right consultant for you." The shocked look on his face said it all. Consultants clearly had never turned him down. I said with his permission, I would share his customer needs with another consultant more suited for his situation.

As I got up from the oversized leather chair, I shook his hand. Had I just turned down business I needed? As I walked through the bank's lobby, I thought about who might be the consultant the President would respect. Stan immediately came to mind. Stan was a tough, 55-year-old Scotsman who no doubt could take the bank President on the golf course and help him realize being a part of the effort was essential to any improvements. The bank President would definitely not call Stan "sweetie."

Stan had recruited me out of academia. He loved nothing better than this kind of challenge. So back in my office, I called Stan. Still angry, I said, "I have an asshole for you to work with that needs bringing out of the 1950s." Stan laughed as I told him what had happened. My simple business strategy for success was born. I do not take on work where I cannot help the client deliver actual improvements, and I don't knowingly work with assholes.

Why was this simple business strategy so successful? As a leader, you must look at your own behaviors first as the root of what needs improving. No amount of coaching or feedback can change values rooted in a lack of integrity and respect.

A leader must want to learn and grow with employees. You can lead a horse to water, but you cannot make the horse thirsty. I try to work with clients with integrity and who engage honestly about improvements. I have never taken on a client whom I did not honestly believe I could help achieve transformational change. Working with the best leaders I could find has made all the difference in my life, both professionally and personally.

You may be thinking I wasn't courageous because I did not confront the President with his "sweetie" comments. For one instant, I thought maybe I could work a miracle. I remembered my first consulting mentor, Dr. June Gallessich's advice: "Always take your clients where they are and guide them, so they take themselves where they need to be."[10]

Because the President adamantly refused to engage in the effort, there was no opportunity for me to guide him. If I had taken on this project, it would have been like rearranging the deck chairs on the *Titanic*: a lot of activity, but no improvement. Because I was "sweetie" to him, a young woman in a man's career in 1986, no coaching from me would be taken seriously by him.

I genuinely wanted to help make this organization a better place for employees and customers. Believe me, nothing would have been more satisfying than to personally rip into this person. But it wasn't the right thing to do, and it would not have created the potential for genuine systemic improvement in him, the employees or the organization. Satisfying as it would have been in the moment, it would have purely been an ego response. My mother always taught me to "never respond in kind, be better than they are, rise above, and take the high road."

Being the real deal means being willing to pay the price for courage every day. All organizations, no matter how big or small, must have zero tolerance for "sweetie"-type behaviors. We need cultures of honesty and humility that are healthy workplaces. We need to demand engaging and inspiring workplaces where each day we can make a positive difference.

"Between stimulus and response, there is a space. In that space lies our freedom and our power to choose our response. In our response lies our growth and our happiness." [11]

~ VICTOR FRANKL ~

What Does It Take?

What does it take to find and use your unique leadership voice? Courage. What does it take for you to sing in your own key rather than changing to try to sound like someone else? Courage. What does it take to ask for the unvarnished truth about your leadership behaviors? Courage. What does it take for a follower to stand up to the leader when the leader is wrong? Courage. What does it take for each of us to admit mistakes and ask for help in learning how to improve? Courage. Yes, courage is needed to be vulnerable and face our fears.

Talk Is Cheap—What Are You Going to Do About It?

Many of us thought with the election of the first Black President of the United States a new era of racial and social justice had begun. We were wrong. In 2021, White supremacists and White nationalists according to FBI Director Christopher Wray posed the greatest violent terror threat to America.[12]

When you are the first and the only Black, the only woman, the only openly gay, the only Asian American, the only Native American in a room full of White men, courage takes on new meaning. Diversity and inclusion are hot topics in American workplaces in 2023. However, the systemic challenges facing creating equality for all, not just for some, are deeper, wider and rawer emotionally than many want to admit.

The Banana Peel Dilemma

Stepping off the giant stage in a huge outdoor arena to thundering applause, this leader had knocked the first speech at the company's annual international sales event out of the park. So, this is how it finally feels to be a rock star as a leader. Feeling validated after years of hard work, the leader walks back for what seemed like miles to the parking area. Arriving at the car, the leader found the car covered with banana peels. What? Was this vandalism? Was this some sort of crazy hazing for being the newest senior sales leader?

Driving the car to the nearest car wash, flashes from the speech, the warm welcome by the CEO, the cheers during the speech, then seeing the banana peels even on the door handle just did not fit. Was this how new senior leaders were welcomed or something else?

The leader's first reaction to seeing the banana peels was shock, then fear, then anger. Being the first and only Black on the senior team, this was not what this leader had expected in 2019. Racism was in full view, no subtlety about the message being sent. Already "walking on eggshells" being the first African American on an all-White team, just made the salt in the wound burn deeper.

"If you can only be tall because someone else is on their knees, then you have a serious problem. And my feeling is white people have a very, very serious problem. They should start thinking about what they can do about it. Take me out of it." [13]

~ TONI MORRISON ~

Pulitzer Prize-Winning Novelist and Nobel Prize in Literature 1993

What would you do in this situation? Well, report it of course. Would you really? Would you take the risk, even when to this day acknowledging this racist act of intimidation would label you as an angry Black person? In 2023 many think all people would be appalled by this act. We optimistically expect whoever did this would be found and fired. I so wish this was true. The reality was and still is in far too many workplaces, to raise a racist claim is a career-limiting action. Sad, depressing, infuriating and still true.

We are just now starting to have "the real talk" about issues of equality. Diversity and Inclusion efforts have for too long been check-the-box activities for leaders in organizations. Changing the systemic racial and sexual biases in organizations is just in its infancy in many organizations. Too many leaders think it's a "Human Resources issue." Racism is a leadership issue, a business issue, and a fundamental organizational issue starting at the Board of Directors' level and permeating throughout all organizational levels and jobs.

I confess (as I was taught confession is good for the soul) I thought of myself as "getting" the subtle and not-so-subtle challenges of sexism and racism until I came face-to-face with overt racism in for-profit and not-for-profit organizations.

As a consultant, I told a Board of Directors their longtime Chief Marketing Officer (CMO) had made racial slurs. The CMO also tried to make a Black peer look like a performance problem when the person was not a performance problem. After providing the data on the CMO's actions, I gave my recommendation to fire the CMO based on legal and moral grounds. The Board decided on early retirement for the CMO for fear of angering anyone. Enough said.

I just recently learned about Viola Liuzzo, a civil rights activist in 1965 and the only White woman to be murdered by the Ku Klux Klan for her civil rights activities. According to Biography. com: "Viola Gregg Liuzzo travelled to Alabama in March 1965 to help the Southern Christian Leadership Conference—led by Rev. Martin Luther King, Jr.—with its efforts to register African American voters in Selma. Not long after her arrival, Liuzzo was murdered by members of the Ku Klux Klan while driving a Black man from Montgomery to Selma. She was the only known White female killed during the civil rights movement."[14] Viola Liuzzo paid the price for what she must have said, "It's everyone's fight."[15]

People of color and women of all colors do not need more courage. They have endured, persevered, worked three times as hard, jumped higher, and achieved more just to be considered for a leadership position. Let's be clear, the label as a token has taken its toll. Truth needs to be spoken. People of color and women are at the table because they have more than earned leadership jobs.

What I know is, leading as a Black woman in a White male-dominated environment takes courage beyond what it takes for a White woman in the same situation. Make no mistake, all women must fight and overachieve to get a seat at the table still. Women of color face both racism and sexism. Despite how hard it has been for me as a White woman fighting sexism, women leaders of color have had it exponentially harder.

Inspiring Courageous Leaders

No matter what your politics, you must admire the actions of the Senior Senator from Minnesota. She not only launched her Presidential bid in a snowstorm, but had the courage to put what was best for her country first before her own political ambitions.

Senator Amy Klobuchar pulled out of consideration for the 2020 Vice Presidential nominee for the Democratic ticket. This act no doubt was tough, as she had worked as hard as anyone to be the Presidential nominee, and this is the next best job.

What is inspiring about what Senator Klobuchar did next was what she said in her public announcement. Live—in person—for all the world to see and hear, she had the courage to do what she felt was right for her country. Klobuchar says she called Biden and told him, "I truly believe . . . this is a moment to put a woman of color on that ticket. There are so many incredibly qualified women. But if you want to heal this nation right now, my party, yes, but our nation, this is sure a hell of a way to do it."[16]

Senator Klobuchar met the moment as a leader. Courage is needed to advocate for a woman of color to be Vice President. Unselfish, country over self, these leadership actions are all too rare in so many political leaders. Senator Amy Klobuchar did the right thing, in the right way, for the right reason and set an inspiring example of *Being the Real Deal.*

The then-Senator Kamala Harris said Presidential candidate Joe Biden had the "audacity" to pick her as his running mate. Courage was demonstrated by both leaders as Biden and Harris were elected and sworn in as President and Vice President of the United States of America. As the first woman and woman of color to serve as Vice President—history was made.

Vice President Harris exhibits daily courage and grace as vicious vitriol toward her explodes daily on social media. She proudly proclaims, "While I may be the first woman in this office, I will not be the last."[17]

Now we must have the courage to make equality not a single historic event but an everyday experience for all people. Vice President Harris is a historic first; however, she is leading as an inspiring courageous example of *Being the Real Deal* because she fearlessly speaks truth to power.

Keep Growing!

1. What are examples of courage demonstrating how you were "willing to pay the price" for the integrity principle?

2. How do you know if people experience you the same in public as in private as a leader?

3. Describe how your actions as a leader set an example that inspires others to act with courage and integrity.

4. How do you manage the simultaneous feelings of courage and fear? How can you increase your ability to be vulnerable, and make vulnerability one of your leadership strengths?

5. As leaders, we have almost daily opportunities to try to solve systemic problems. What are you doing to boldly address systemic racism and sexism within your organization, community, friends and family?

"Anyone who claims to be a leader must speak like a leader. That means speaking with integrity and truth." [18]

~ Vice President Kamala Harris ~
Vice President of the United States of America

CHAPTER SIX

Endings and Beginnings

"The axe forgets; the tree remembers." [1]

~ AFRICAN PROVERB ~

Stumped

Even the mightiest oak trees can be cut down. Even the best and brightest leaders face both the beginning of their leadership roles and the ending of their leadership roles. One leader's ending is another leader's beginning. We have in the past treated these as separate actions, but they are, in fact, intertwined.

When you cut down an oak tree you may think you have removed it. However, if the stump and roots remain, the oak tree can regrow. Ending a leader's role does not ensure transformative change will take place when the new leader is faced with stump and roots removal.

Does announcing a leader's departure automatically turn the leader into a lame duck? Yes, it does, according to conventional wisdom. The leader becomes a placeholder until the new leader is on the job. Unconventional wisdom says leaving a leadership role can be a bigger opportunity for transformational change than beginning a leadership role.

According to Sally Blount, President and CEO, Catholic Charities, Archdioceses of Chicago, and former Dean at Northwestern's Kellogg School of Management, the last 90 days in a leadership role are more important than the first 90 days. "Much has been written about the first 90 days at a job. Interestingly, there is no corollary thinking about the last 90 days. How a tenure ends will always be more accessible in people's memories than the impressions created at the start."[2]

Leaders who are *Being the Real Deal* refuse the conventional "lame duck" status. They continue to do what is needed so the next person in the leadership role can be even more successful than they have been. They have the courage to move their team and the organization forward, even as they announce their plans to depart the organization. They lead despite the forces trying to make them irrelevant. Following this unconventional wisdom, leaders enable their team and organization to be more successful once the new leader arrives.

Challenging conventional wisdom's gigantic gravitational pull to do what has always been done requires a deep commitment to your team and the company's success. Unconventional wisdom says removing leadership obstacles—yes, removing stumps and deeply rooted problems *prior* to leaving, enabling your successor to be more successful than you—are the exception not the rule in far too many leadership transitions. *Being the Real Deal* requires leading with unconventional wisdom.

A Case for Leading With Unconventional Wisdom

As the new Global Chief Information Officer (CIO), James wanted to transform the role of Information Technology (IT) within his company. The IT team had always been treated as a support staff expense item rather than as a strategic business partner. James knew IT was core to the company's success and growth. He also knew information technology must be a competitive advantage integral to the business' growth strategy. However, his leadership efforts to transform IT ran into a brick wall. How had it come to this?

The First 90 Days

Excitement and optimism were in the air as James accepted the formidable task of developing the company's first global IT function and processes. The company had a complex set of global businesses operating in over 100 countries with 50,000-plus employees. The sheer size combined with international and local legacy IT systems presented enormous information technology challenges.

The importance of "Big Data" and the need to create new technological capabilities was every business leader's hot topic. The company's strategy was for IT to become a competitive advantage. All the company's leaders were in absolute verbal agreement with the IT strategy. James was tasked with a complex global innovation effort. With the right resources and leadership, the IT transformation would position the company for guaranteed long-term success.

The role of Global CIO was new without an established global technology governance model. As the company's freshly minted first Global CIO, this young leader, who had been promoted from within, was literally staring at a blank sheet of paper for his job description. To add to the challenge, the business' culture was rooted in IT's role as a transactional expense to business partners, not as a strategic business partner with profit-making potential.

James was a top talent with integrity, a dedicated team player, and an extremely experienced IT leader who knew the business. He was the natural choice for Global CIO. He had earned the new position of Global CIO by delivering real improvements and building great teams. Clearly, he had the expertise and the leadership talent to build a global IT organization working as a partner with business leaders. He had a sterling reputation, and people genuinely liked and trusted him, both personally and professionally.

Developing and executing a new global IT strategy while simultaneously building a global IT team were big challenges, even for a star talent like James. Just to keep things interesting, the company made its biggest acquisition ever, which had complex integration demands and substantial IT savings targets.

If anyone could handle these huge challenges, it was James. The CFO and James' direct boss, Virgil, believed in James' leadership talents. Virgil consistently urged James to "lead through influence" to create needed changes. Virgil set high expectations for James as an organizational superstar who everyone thought could achieve dramatic improvements in a short time frame. "Drive change through influence" was the coaching James received from his boss Virgil, from me, his external executive coach, and from his business partners. Because of his collaborative style and technology expertise, all thought the new CIO would naturally excel in his new undefined CIO role.

Strategy Agreement vs. Implementing Strategy

At the highest levels, from the CEO through the far reaches of this massive global organization, the global IT strategy developed and championed by James appeared to be 100 percent aligned. The leadership chorus throughout the company sounded in harmony. Information Technology and Business Units were to be true business partners in every sense of the word.

James worked collaboratively with business leaders who agreed with him in meetings, then later blamed IT whenever their business did not meet their financial targets. James and the IT teams began being shot at from all sides. At the same time, James was being coached to "drive change through influence." Leading from any chair works theoretically if the leader is "talented enough" and has the right values. All had bought into this "drive change through influence" leadership model.

Blinded by the Light

Falling into the trap of believing a talented leader could use his/her influence successfully despite challenging obstacles is more common than you might think. Somehow, the heroic leader myth, the knight in shining armor who single-handedly overthrows the army of obstacles, had taken hold. I shared my coaching mistake directly with James after regrettably seeing it through the 20/20 clear lens of hindsight.

As James' executive coach, I, too, had bought into the idea that James' talent as a leader was enough to achieve success. No one questioned whether he could lead difficult transformational change with only influence as his power base. Overcoming the structural, cultural, and reward-system barriers to transformation proved to require more than talent and influence.

Even the most seasoned Global CIO would have struggled given the systemic obstacles. IT was not at the table at the highest decision-making level to make the case to hold business partners accountable. James had great difficulty recruiting the team he needed. The IT strategy was "spot-on," but the processes, structure, rewards, and the company's culture blocked IT and business leaders from working as partners at every turn.

Business leaders were rewarded for making their numbers, not investing in IT. Short-term, not long-term thinking prevailed in the business units. If the outcome negatively affected the P&L in the short term, the short term won.

To paraphrase many others, "Execution eats strategy for breakfast." Jim Skinner, Non-Executive Director, Walgreens Boots Alliance, Inc., and retired CEO of McDonald's, reminded me in an interview with him, "Face it, Vicky, nothing is ever successful until after it's been implemented."[3]

James had worked all the angles. No matter who the Global CIO was, she or he would have encountered the same obstacles, frustrations, and blame game. The business leaders' refrain was all the same: "If only IT could deliver more with less cost, the businesses could hit their numbers." Virgil did a forceful job presenting the IT case for innovation and investment. Even though James was the Global CIO, he was not at the table for crucial discussions and decisions.

"A bad system will beat a good person every time." [4]

~ W. Edwards Deming ~

Words vs. Actions

James became engulfed in the trenches with the new acquisition IT problems. Without leverage and positional power, James' efforts to drive transformational change across the organization were blocked. The businesses continued treating IT as a transactional expense. Business leaders said they believed IT is the business driver of profits but acted as they always had, treating IT as a costly service.

Everyone struggled. Fighting each day for limited success was at best frustrating and extremely stressful. Long, hard hours with little or no rewards makes for an "I do not love what I am doing" feeling each morning when coming to work. Worst of all, the battles had taken their toll on James' sterling reputation. A prominent, powerful business partner began openly questioning James' credibility.

James had many advocates and supporters, but he lost control of the narrative being told throughout senior management. Others were telling only their part of the story. Politics, in the worst sense of the word, became the new game of choice by IT's harshest critics. Their motives seemed obvious. If the focus was on IT's shortcomings, then their business' lack of performance would not be in the spotlight.

James refused to play political games or compromise his values and integrity. He was advised by Virgil not to go head-to-head with the business leader who was his loudest critic, and I agreed. It would have been political suicide to take on his harshest critic who was not telling the entire story. James faced a high probability of losing the political battle, resulting in being immediately fired.

Half of James wanted the showdown, the other half knew the stakes were too high. He desperately wanted to get to the root of the business problems. James did not want to desert his team and leave in a fiery blaze of political brinkmanship. If he lost, he and his team would pay dearly. Better to continue the influence fight and at least still be in the game. From that moment on the die was cast. James knew in his heart by not playing hardball, he had "crossed the Rubicon."[5] Talent had not triumphed.

Robert Lane, then-Chairman and CEO of Deere & Company, in a 2008 interview explained to me why talent alone is not enough:

"Talent, just pure talent, isn't sufficient. Because we could have great geniuses join us here, but if they aren't pulling together with the rest of the team, it's counterproductive. We'd much rather have 50,000 people pulling in the right direction, pulling

together, than ten brilliant people pulling in opposite directions. And so, getting the team to pull together, work together . . . It's talent that works together—that to me is the 'secret sauce.'"[6]

Despite James' and his boss' best efforts, the business and IT leaders were not pulling together as business partners. The day finally came when James and his boss had used all their respective political capital. James had done all he could do. Both tried to make it work, both were high-integrity, top-rated leaders. All of us had contributed to the failure to transform IT and business leaders into true business partners.

Despite the personally painful reality for James and his boss, they knew a leadership change was required. Decision made. James would leave the company. The perfunctory email went out. James was leaving to pursue other career interests but would stay on until his successor could be found. James went from a highly talented and compelling leader to instantly being "ineffective"—a lame duck on his way out the door.

Typically, this is where the story ends. James becomes a lame duck with people being polite but dismissive of his leadership efforts. James disengages to totally focus externally on his next career opportunity. The IT change efforts and organization are put on hold waiting for the new leader's arrival.

It would take any new leader 6 months to learn what was happening and then another 10-plus months to start implementing needed changes. Over a year of precious time would be lost in even getting to the implementation of the global IT strategy all professed was critical for the company's success.

Surprisingly, this is not how the story ends. Ironically, by announcing his leaving, James became the influential transformational leader the business needed, and he leveraged the talents all saw in him.

The Last 90 Days

What did James do to make his announced departure an opportunity for transformational change?

Although some questioned the "real reason" he was leaving, James was sincerely happy. He saw this as a genuine career opportunity for himself. Colleagues commented, "I have not ever seen James this happy." There were "no bridges burned" on either side.

Using leaving as a platform for improvement was James' idea. He would not be a lame duck for the 6 months it took to find his replacement. "This is not who I am as a leader, nor was it going to be the legacy I left for my IT team," said James. No one was in a better position than James to understand the obstacles, or the changes needed for the new leader to be successful in the Global CIO leader role. James knew the roots of the problems, and that if both the roots and stump were not removed, then the ground would not be clear for new growth. The next leader would be faced with the roots and stump that would regenerate the same old problems causing the tree to be cut down again.

Value-driven leaders like James find a way to make a difference even at personal sacrifice. "Not taking it personally" is always a challenge. Moving past the personal and focusing on what was best for the business was part of James' DNA. Sounds simple enough, but how many of us have seen leaders in the same situation act very differently?

Sally Blount notes, "Despite its importance, the truth is that many senior executives botch their exits."[7] Many exits aren't the needed platforms for change because of the leaving leader's behavior. Bruised egos slam the door on opportunities to fix things.

We too often put a mantle of failure on one individual when organizational failure and success involve many people. As Githesh Ramamurthy, Chairman and CEO of CCIS advised me, "The problem in many organizations is success has many parents, but failure has only one."[8]

Caring Creates Commitment for Rooting Out Systemic Problems

James cared deeply for his team, which was a key driver for his refusal to be a lame duck. "If you care about your team, you want to create an environment where after you are gone the team can be successful." James knew he was not the root problem. "I really wanted to solve this business problem, and that gave me the energy to be highly engaged. I never changed how I worked with my team."

Another critical success factor was Virgil's (James' boss) buy-in to "getting to root causes and solving the problem now—not waiting." Virgil never stopped believing in James as a credible leader. James lobbied hard to get an external consulting engagement ahead of the arrival of the new Global CIO. Virgil bought into the concept, as this would drive a better business outcome rather than waiting. James became an advocate to his boss and the CEO for not waiting to get to the root causes of the obstacles to IT's global success.

James, Virgil, and the CEO went against the common operating principle most organizations follow. Typically, no changes are made until the successor is in place and has months to assess the situation. So, the organization loses almost an entire year waiting for changes all agree are needed. This is a huge opportunity cost for organizations. Successors spend precious time and other resources focused on setting the stage for success when needed changes should be made before he or she takes the job.

What Were the Personal Drivers for James to Achieve Difficult Changes Before He Left?

James: "There were two main drivers for me: first, caring about the team, and second, not wanting to be a lame duck creating a leadership vacuum and a non-productive environment for six months. I wanted a positive working environment the entire time I was leading my team and afterward. Equally important to me was building the solutions enabling IT to be true business partners in the future. Creating a successful future state for IT became my critical leadership mission. Having a critical goal with time pressure to get it done enabled me and others to engage authentically on mission-critical real business work."

Why Did James Care About His Successor's Success?

James: "I didn't know my successor at the time. The biggest driver was to create what was needed for the team to have real business success. I had a good sense of the core dynamics resisting IT being business leaders as equals. I saw an opportunity to shine a light on changes required for IT and the business to truly partner for the best outcomes for the company."

James: "Candidly, I think there was also an element of personal validation through it as well. It took the external consulting team, the CEO, my boss, and me to get others to understand the set of broader dynamics making it difficult for IT to be successful. It became about creating the conditions that needed to be in place for IT to be effective. When we stopped the blame game and looked at the issues through the same lens, it was clear this was not a James problem.

The broader structural problem was collectively identified, and senior management was positioned to fix the structural problems. Having me leave became an opportunity for change. Despite my great working relationship with my boss the CFO, Information Technology did not have a direct seat at the table with the executive team. The operating model needed to be one where IT was on equal footing with the business with direct communication and access to real-time decision-making with the CEO. There were several important things that came together that made me relevant all the way to the end. People knew I was designing the future; therefore, I was still important. Also, I maintained a strong personal connection with team members by continuing to lead until my last day on the job—so not a lame duck."

What James and I Learned

~Decision-making power is required.
Leading through influence is great if others have the same values, rewards, and goals. Influence, however, has its limits. Without a direct seat at the decision-making table, resistance to change often wins. We love stories where the hero single-handedly moves mountains. Transformational change takes considerable formal power with all leaders engaged and pulling in the same direction.

~ Information Technology is the business.
Strategy can be brilliant, but it must be integrated into the business. IT drives business strategy for all companies in the digital age. IT must be business partners in every sense of the word.

~ Reinventing yourself in your current job is not always possible.
There is a point where a leader cannot change the narrative because too many negative comments have defined you to others. Once integrity is tarnished—the damage has been done.

~ Control the narrative or others will.
Stories that are mostly true are repeated, but more and more of the negative can get attached to a leader's reputation. As the stories continue with no strong rebuttal, the negative starts sticking, and it quickly snowballs with half-true information being treated as fact until a huge avalanche is triggered. The effect on one's internal reputation can be devastating.

~ Talent alone is never sufficient.
Resources, processes, decision-making power, rewards, and consequences must be aligned for talented leaders to achieve innovations.

~ Treat strategy and execution as one effort.
People often agree on the strategy, as we love great ideas. However, when asked to do hard things, people can be unwilling to pay the price for the improvement. Remember, "Nothing is successful until after it's executed."[9]

~ Leaving provides a big opportunity for change.
James, his boss—CFO—and the CEO seized the moment by not waiting for the next leader to drive needed changes. Leading so your legacy is one of integrity, innovation, and setting up others for success means never accepting being a lame-duck leader.

~ To rise above "taking it personally" requires a strong, humble, Real Deal leader.
It takes an exceptionally strong, high-integrity, and humble person—yes, a leader *Being the Real Deal* to rise above "taking it personally" and genuinely care more about the team and the business than his/her own ego needs.

~ Talent can blind you to the difficulties of leading innovation.
Talent can blind those closest to a gifted leader (boss and coach) to the enormous requirements for success in addition to the leader's talents. Success and failure are team and organizational activities.

Keep Growing!

1. What do you need to do in your current leadership role to sow seeds for success for whoever will follow you as leader?

2. What are you doing to develop other leaders in your organization?

3. How do you get highly talented individual leaders to pull together to do what is best for the entire business?

4. When "politics" turns personal and people's integrity is falsely challenged, what do individual leaders do to call out self-serving leaders?

5. If you had been in James' position, what would you have done differently?

"Make your last days leading your team your best leadership efforts creating a legacy of adding value every day." [10]

~ JAMES ~
Global CIO

Chronic Student

"You see, the tough part is you have to crack yourself open if you really want to learn and grow." [1]

~ Dr. Vicky Gordon ~

Growing From an Acorn to an Oak Tree Requires Changing

We, humans, are cracked open to learn and grow from our very beginnings—like an acorn. As babies, we learn everything by satisfying our natural curiosity. We learn by experiencing the world as we learn to crawl, then walk, then run. As we listen, look, touch, taste and smell our environment—we learn. Watch young children as they learn by playing; it's all about the joy of learning while exploring and engaging with others. We keep trying new behaviors over and over while giving ourselves more energy for each effort.

As young children, we delight in asking question after question to adults. We start our lives in the fearless pursuit of learning. As Albert Einstein admitted, "I have no special talent; I am only passionately curious."[2] Yes, we are all little Einsteins—passionately curious chronic students. Keeping our childlike curiosity vibrant is key to a lifelong learning journey.

More Important Than Money

Inspiring leaders crave learning opportunities. While sitting in a rising star's corporate office one day, I listened as this young, charismatic leader analyzed what seemed on the surface like an amazing career opportunity. A company had offered the young leader a starting base salary of 1 million dollars (which did not include a bonus) to join their senior leadership team. This offer would have substantially increased the person's current salary. This was and still is a hell of a lot of money—especially for someone so young. The company's job offer was beyond tempting.

Most would have jumped at such an opportunity. However, the young leader was wise beyond his years. He said, "Vicky—if something is too good to be true, it must have some not-so-obvious downsides." For the next several hours we discussed all aspects of the company, the job offer, and his personal and professional goals. He identified the short- and long-term reasons to either accept or reject the offer. This simple, analytical exercise identified the positives and negatives of this career opportunity.

The top positive was—you guessed it—the 1 million dollar base salary. The top negative—the job opportunity was a dead-end job with no potential for growth. The young leader knew how to do this job and could hit the ground running. Seductive as the money was, my client decided to turn down the offer. As he explained to me, "No amount of money can substitute for a job where I learn, grow, and develop as a business leader. I will make 10 times that amount if I take a less lucrative job now which positions me to learn how to be a global CEO and Board Chair."

In fact, that is exactly the career path this young leader chose. The individual became a successful global business leader: admired, and sought after by business, governmental and philanthropic organizations. My client knew who he was from the inside out. As he said to me, "If I take the 1 million dollar job, I will leave in a few years because I will get bored and not challenged to keep learning—I will never take a dead-end job." To the executive recruiting firm's shock, the young leader said no thank you to the money. Instead, he pursued challenging growth opportunities, preferring to play career chess, not checkers.

"The cure for boredom is curiosity. There is no cure for curiosity."[3]

~ ELLEN PARR ~

Being the Smartest Is Not Always Wise

Most of us dislike it when people present themselves as know-it-alls. One of the traps for intellectually gifted leaders is they get to the answers to problems faster than most. Showing that you are the smartest person in the room does not engage or inspire others.

Collaboration and teamwork inspire others. Leaders can energize others by asking questions instead of giving answers. The typical human response to the "let me show you how smart I am" behavior is silence. As we sit in silence listening to the leader pontificate, we think to ourselves: "If you are so smart, why haven't you already solved this problem? Why are we wasting our time if you are going to take the ball and run without us?" A case in point:

The new CEO was brilliant and friendly. He was highly respected by his direct reports. He became frustrated with his direct reports because no one brought up new ideas to him individually or in his weekly staff meetings. He said to me, "I just don't get it. Why aren't people knocking down my door with ideas and issues? No one comes in and says, 'I have a new idea and I think we ought to do this differently.'"

What the CEO didn't see was how his own behavior was blocking the exact behavior he wanted from his direct reports.

Every time someone brought up an idea in a staff meeting, he would immediately analyze and dissect the idea. Before anyone else had a chance to comment, he would tell the group what he thought ought to be done and forcefully begin assigning tasks. In staff meetings, when the CEO started outsmarting everyone and dictating tasks, "It was like all the oxygen was being sucked out of the room," a direct report shared with me.

It didn't take long before his direct reports just waited for him to give them the answer and then tell them exactly what to do. They literally stopped bringing up ideas and issues. The CEO had trained them not to take initiative. More devastating was how his leadership behaviors had extinguished his direct reports' curiosity. I advised him, "Give others a safe space to take the initiative. If you want others' ideas and opinions, then listen first. Do not immediately provide your analysis. Ask thoughtful questions enabling the team to ask questions, be creative and curious. Have them do the analysis together rather than doing the analysis for them. Stop demonstrating that you are the smartest person in the room. Your leadership job is to get other people to demonstrate how smart they are."

With this change in his behavior, ideas and information began slowly flowing. Over time the direct reports even began challenging the CEO's ideas by asking tough questions. By changing how he was leading, the CEO changed how others were following.

The Power of "I Don't Know" to Inspire

Dr. Paul Brandes, one of my professors at UNC-Chapel Hill, would often say, "The most dangerous person I know is a newly minted Ph. D. Why? Because when asked a question in the individual's specialty the person is often afraid to say three simple words: I don't know."

Leaders who fail to question are, in my experience, also dangerous. Yes, dangerous. They lead by signaling "it's their way or the highway." Courage to question requires humility. Admitting you do not know exemplifies vulnerability and humility behaviors. Just because you have the title of Ph. D., CEO, leadership coach or team leader does not mean you know it all. What do "I don't know" behaviors have to do with inspiration? Wistawa Szymborska, Polish Poet and 1996 Nobel laureate, in his Nobel speech explains how the learning journey and not knowing creates inspiration.

"Inspiration is not the exclusive privilege of poets or artists generally. There is, has been, and will always be a certain group of people whom inspiration visits. It's made up of all those who've consciously chosen their calling and do their job with love and imagination. It may include doctors, teachers, gardeners—and I could list a hundred more professions. Their work becomes one continuous adventure as long as they manage to keep discovering new challenges in it. Difficulties and setbacks never quell their curiosity. A swarm of new questions emerges from every problem they solve. Whatever inspiration is, it's born from a continuous 'I don't know.'"[4]

Always an A Student

As one of the top candidates in the succession plan for a global corporation, Harry exuded an intellectual confidence that comes from always being the A student, both in school and in each of his jobs. Bright, strategic, result-driven, high achiever—he had gotten to this place in his career through hard work and by making certain results were achieved. The Vice President of Human Resources and the President both thought it would be the right move for me to be Harry's leadership coach, since I was the President's coach going through the same 360 Feedback Leadership Development and Coaching process.

From having coached CEOs and succession candidates successfully with other clients, I thought my work with Harry would accelerate his development process as it had in my past work. I was wrong. In this case, what I did not know was this scenario with Harry did not provide the safety he required to genuinely engage in self-reflection and acknowledgment of the leadership behaviors needing development efforts.

Safety provides the fertile ground for people to explore, test, and make mistakes while building leadership strengths. Far too often, leaders are thrown into the deep end of the pool without the opportunity to learn how to swim in unfamiliar, choppy waters. The "sink or swim" leadership development model is one of the worst methods of developing leaders.

As I was writing about what I did not know in this situation, I was reminded of my stay in northern California at a wildlife preserve. Zebras roamed freely on the preserve. Hearing the hooves hitting the ground, and then seeing the wild striped animals charging at me, my heart raced as I bolted to safety, never allowing myself to get close to the frightening animals. I would literally shake from the adrenaline rush of fear of not being safe. What I did not know was that fear and the need for safety were exactly what Harry felt every time I showed up at his office door for a leadership coaching session.

Harry had gotten to a prized place as the top succession candidate to become the next President. Harry did not trust the coaching situation, as he would have to defend himself from Dr. Vicky's piercing eyes and cutting questions. Having the President's coach as his coach did not provide the safety Harry needed to let his guard down. He would not risk having a coach who might surface his weaknesses. Harry showed strength by always being an A student and creating his own safety net.

Both Harry and I were triggered by each other, and we were both hooked into past stories of our need to prove we were "good enough." Hindsight and reflection are essential learning tools, but they are afterthoughts. Both are essential for growth, but neither can rescue you in the moment when you are trapped by hooks and triggers.

The use of coaches and 360 feedback processes have morphed into routine parts of leadership development. It takes an extraordinary level of trust for individuals to have faith in you as their leadership coach and to disclose confidential information.

I had gotten input from the President, Harry's peers and direct reports about Harry's strengths and development needs. I was hooked by the President's input and made a hasty judgment. Given my experience and the partnership I had with the President, I thought I was perfectly positioned to quickly help Harry as his coach. This was a reaction driven by my ego—let me show the President just how great a coach I am by having Harry quickly demonstrate real behavioral improvements.

My first coaching session with Harry was a mutual admiration society meeting with both of us expressing how great it would be to work together. We genuinely liked and respected each other. Harry had decided that, given I had a Ph. D., he could be a brilliant student, get straight A's from his coach, and all would be impressed, including his boss. All he had to do was ace the steps in the 360 feedback and coaching process, check the box done, and then be the President's number one succession candidate. I did not agree with Harry's analytical linear approach to the leadership development process—gather the data, construct the development plan, and then be done with coaching. This was the beginning of the end of our working together.

Harry's 360 feedback data was full of examples of all his strengths—strategic mindset, business acumen—all the things the President was looking for in a successor. He was already "good enough"; he was at the leadership table. Yet all he had to do was let his guard down—be vulnerable and open up to me, his boss, and his direct reports. What the President saw as a development need was Harry's being open to learning, being vulnerable and having the humility to engage others in leading rather than directing and controlling. Could Harry for once not be an A student? Could Harry become a leader of leaders and not direct and control? Could he instead engage the leaders on his team? Could he collaborate with his peers instead of competing with them?

So, what are all the things I missed at the beginning of this coaching process? First, Harry did not believe in partnering with a coach. He wanted to know the assignment, complete it and then have me evaluate and grade the assignment. More importantly, we both got hooked by needing to prove we were "good enough." We ended up like the Chinese finger puzzle where we each put one finger in and tried to pull our respective fingers out of the puzzle. We were both pulling in opposite directions. The harder we tried to move the other in our direction, the more stuck we became. To get unstuck in the Chinese finger puzzle both must move toward each other, not away.

The "be vulnerable paradox" is analogous to the "be spontaneous paradox." One cannot "order" a person to be vulnerable. Giving the order takes away the option of genuine vulnerability, just as you cannot order a person to be spontaneous. Both vulnerability and spontaneity require the person to initiate the behavior without being ordered.

I can still feel my frustration of not being able to crack open the learning code with Harry. I should have identified after the first 360 feedback session, seeing the frightened look on his face, like a deer in headlights—Harry did not feel safe with anything but an A grade on his leadership. There was genuine fear of any data saying that he was not an A student.

I shared my failure and my frustrations as Harry's coach with the President. Harry also shared his frustrations with me as his coach with the President and Vice President of Human Resources. Harry got a different coach and still ended up as the number one successor candidate. In fact, Harry has gone on to be an extremely effective President.

What cracks us open to learning and growing? The hardest lessons come when our best efforts fail—the school of hard knocks. We are tested by life's storms that bend us until we almost break. But because of our deep roots, we survive the storm, battered but not uprooted. I learned once again each situation and person is unique. Just because a coaching process has worked in the past for others does not mean it will work in the present situation. Humbled by my mistake with Harry, I now always question how safe leaders will feel with me as their coach.

Intellectual Curiosity Required

Great masters of their professions have always known learning is core to their greatness. Take Michelangelo, who at age 87 is reported to have said "Ancora imparo," which is Italian for "Still, I am learning."[5] Or the legendary cellist Pablo Casals when asked why he continued to practice at age 83, "Because I think I am making progress," he replied.[6] Then there is the 95-year-old Angela Álvarez who won a Latin Grammy for Best New Artist and is the oldest person to ever win a Latin Grammy.[7] Susan Crown, Chairman and Founder at SCE, advises leaders, "You never get to a point where you know everything you need to know. That's the real deal—intellectual curiosity about everything."[8]

I have worked as a coach with a wide range of individuals who are considered high potential, fast-track rising stars. The one characteristic every one of these individuals has in common irrespective of position, industry, background, age, race or sex, is the insatiable desire to always be learning. When they stop learning, they start looking elsewhere for jobs. They want jobs where they can continue to learn and grow as professionals and personally.

Leading is an exercise in constant learning. As leaders we need the humility to say "I don't know"; the courage to ask questions and the skill to listen with an open mind. Reading, watching others, getting coaching and mentoring, taking academic courses all are helpful. However, there is no substitute for learning by doing. Greg Brown, Chairman and CEO of Motorola Solutions, Inc., shared in an interview with me his simple yet profound leadership mantra—please note the order of these behaviors.

"Listen, Learn, then Lead" [9]

~ GREG BROWN ~

Chairman and Chief Executive Officer of Motorola Solutions, Inc.

Keep Growing!

1. What are you doing to keep learning as a leader?

2. What inspires you to keep asking questions?

3. How do you demonstrate your humility and vulnerability as you continue to grow in your leadership capabilities?

4. What sparks your intellectual curiosity?

5. What do you have to "crack open" to continue growing as a leader?

"If everything was perfect, you would never learn and would never grow." [10]

~ BEYONCE ~

CHAPTER EIGHT

Everyone Has a Dream

"If your actions create a legacy that inspires others to dream more, learn more, do more and become more, then, you are an excellent leader." [1]

~ DOLLY PARTON ~

Singer, Actor, Philanthropist

Dreams

One of the human truths is—we all have dreams. We all aspire "to become" from our earliest years. We have dreams of becoming our own version of a majestic wise oak tree reaching always upward toward the sunlight. *Being the Real Deal* requires you to inspire others to "dream more, learn more, do more, become more"[2] as a leader.

Adults nag children with their proverbial question—"What do you want to be when you grow up?" Truthfully, I am still wrestling with this question, as we can and do become many different things throughout our lives. Then as "we gather more years,"[3] we develop our "bucket list" of dreams—things we want to achieve before we die.

Remember this as a leader: Everyone has a dream—everyone on your team, everyone in your organization, everyone in your family, everyone in your community, country, yes, everyone in the world has a dream. Your job as a leader is to understand those dreams and do whatever is in your power to help as many people as you can achieve their dreams. Leadership is about helping others be successful.

What Would Warren Bennis, Ph. D., Say?

In his 1989 book, *Why Leaders Can't Lead, The Unconscious Conspiracy Continues*, Warren Bennis asks, "Where have all the leaders gone?" We are still asking this question as a country and as a world.

". . . we seem unwilling to use our best qualities at all.
Our best qualities are integrity, dedication, magnanimity,
humility, openness and creativity. These of course are the basic
ingredients of leadership and our unwillingness to tap these
qualities in ourselves explain, to a large extent,
the leadership shortage."[4]

~ WARREN BENNIS ~

Let's be honest. Dr. Bennis's book is just as relevant today, if not more relevant than in 1989. Despite revolutionary changes in technology—the adage "the more things change the more they stay the same" is true about leadership today. We have too many bosses, authoritarian leaders, and too few inspiring leaders embodying Bennis's best qualities. Where have the inspiring leaders gone when we need them the most?

Too many organizational environments are controlled by fear. If people speak up, they fear being fired or not being promoted. Courage is needed to step up—speak our truth and say this isn't working for me and ask: How do we make our world, our country, our community, our company, our schools, our meetings, our work, our families better?

The autocratic leadership style should have died of natural causes years ago. When faced with a toxic environment, we must stand together to clean it up and plant seeds of respect, truth, integrity, humility, transparency, compassion, equality, and freedom.

Yes, we all have dreams, yet far too often dreams become only aspirations without concrete outcomes. Your specific everyday leadership actions are what inspire others to work together to turn their dreams into realities.

Your leadership light must shine so bright you enable others to step into the dark unknown. Just as Captain Kirk and the *Star Trek* team would "bravely go where no others have gone before,"[5] inspiring leaders light the way.

Do you embody hope despite a world engulfed in despair? We can and we must be inspired ourselves as leaders before we can expect others to be inspired. Our grit and determination when fueled by love and compassion keep us starting each new day with hope grounded in the reality "it takes a village"[6] to turn dreams into realities.

"Not everybody can be famous, but everybody can be great because greatness is determined by service . . . You only need a heart full of grace and a soul generated by love."[7]

~ DR. MARTIN LUTHER KING, JR. ~

In his famous "I Have a Dream" speech Dr. Martin Luther King, Jr. gave one of the most inspiring calls to action for freedom, justice, and equality ever given. Dr. King's words were aspirational; however, his leadership actions—nonviolent protests, marches, sit-ins, being jailed, and his mobilization of the civil rights movement in the 1960s in America—are what galvanized a nation to pass transformative civil rights legislation.

I grew up in the segregated South. I saw where crosses were burned in front yards of African Americans who dared to move into "White areas." I know firsthand what courage looks like when individuals literally faced down racism. Dr. King embodied nonviolent principles and practices as he and many others led a nation to face its ugly realities of social injustice and racism.

"I have been to the mountaintop, and I have seen the Promised Land . . . I have a dream today . . . Let us not seek to satisfy our thirst for freedom by drinking from the cup of bitterness and hatred. We must forever conduct our struggle on the high plane of dignity and discipline. We must not allow our creative protest to degenerate into physical violence. Again and again, we must rise to the majestic heights of meeting physical force with soul force . . ." [8]

~ DR. MARTIN LUTHER KING, JR. ~

"I Have a Dream Speech," March on Washington, August 28, 1963

What keeps a leader marching on despite setbacks and challenges—the leader's soul force—are the values rooted deep within. Believing wholeheartedly in the dream keeps us inspired as leaders. Starting inspired at the beginning of achieving a dream is the easier part of the journey.

Staying inspired during transformational challenges tests all leaders. Just the amount and complexity of work required to fundamentally create and implement the new dream can deplete the most passionate person. As I tell my clients, "Leading transformational change is a marathon, not a sprint. Pace yourself, plan watering stations along the way, and remember the final miles require the most energy, grit and grace."

You Are Inspired but Are You Inspiring?

Being inspiring does not require good looks, oratorical skills, a social media following, wealth, power, or fame. Your values are what enable a leader to inspire others. What do some of the most inspiring leaders have in common? They embody the transformation and their values while leading. Their visible leadership behaviors rooted in integrity, passionate purpose, courage, humility, trust, respect, learning and compassion are inspiring.

If you can answer yes to all these questions, then you are inspiring others as you lead them to their "promised land."

* Do you engage others through words and deeds to believe in the dream?

* Do you consistently exhibit a set of behaviors demonstrating your personal engagement?

* Does your team feel your passion for leading a team of dreamers?

* Do you communicate inspiring, engaging messages?

* Do you touch the hearts, heads, and guts of others in ways they, too, feel the commitment, passion, and excitement to join in an inspiring purpose?

* Are you a beacon of light and love?

* Can you elicit light and love from others?

If you can answer yes to all these questions, then you are inspiring others as you lead them to their "promised land."

"I find that people want to do exciting and challenging things. People want to be a part of something special. . . . You can get ordinary people to do extraordinary things with inspiration . . . and it transcends generations." [9]

~ WILLIAM GREEN ~
President, CEO Accenture, 2008 Interview
with Dr. Vicky Gordon

Hope-Filled Environments

Our world is in dire need of leaders who are inspiring because their behaviors are rooted in values of honesty, integrity, courage, and humility. We must build our capacity as leaders to inspire ourselves and be inspiring to others if we are to fundamentally transform our world.

"Acorns need the right soil conditions to germinate and sprout . . . They require loose and moist and nutrient-rich soil in a location that gets plenty of sunlight and rainfall. Given

*these conditions, the acorn will start to germinate and grow
a taproot that pushes deep into the surrounding soil."* [10]

~ ADRIAN GRAHAM ~
Sciencing.com

Leaders are **responsible** for creating an environment where dreams can germinate and grow a taproot. The definition of **responsible** means "having an obligation to do something."[11] Leaders create and maintain the quality of the environment—the climate, the culture, the air and the ground where new dreams can sprout.

The quality of the environment is as critically important to the quality of organizations as is the quality of the air human beings breathe. Just as we cannot live healthy lives breathing polluted air, individuals cannot be inspired "to dream more, learn more, do more"[12] in toxic organizational climates and cultures.

If you are *Being the Real Deal,* you work tirelessly to cultivate a hope-filled culture. Hope is the rich soil, sunlight and water humans require for growth. Leaders are responsible for creating a safe, inspiring ground where dreams, innovations, and ideas can germinate, break through and grow. A nourishing environment, an engaging and uplifting climate; yes—a loving, warm sun-filled place where hope springs eternal.

*"Hope is the thing with feathers
That perches in the soul
And sings the tune without words*

***And never
Stops at all"*** [13]

~ EMILY DICKINSON ~
Hope Is a Thing with Feathers, Stanza I

Everyone's dream has been affected by the first global pandemic in over 100 years. However, those already disadvantaged have and continue to suffer the most. Langston Hughes' powerful poem "Harlem" speaks to the heart of this matter. "What Happens to a Dream Deferred?"[14] Where do we pick up on our dreams deferred? Not where 2020 deferred them, because that place no longer exists. We literally must reimagine our world. The "Great Resignation,"[15] as it has been labeled starting in mid-2021, is the outcome of millions of people reimagining their dream jobs and dream lives.

How do we meet this moment with inspiring leadership? How do we tap into everyone's desire to achieve dreams in the face of so many ongoing, rapidly changing obstacles? When dreams are deferred, or worse, destroyed by forces outside of our individual control, too many lose hope. The negative—the darkness overpowers even the most optimistic of us.

Leading by example with integrity is hardest in the darkest hours. I have never been more concerned in all arenas about what we are doing to develop inspiring leaders rooted in integrity. We must hold all leaders to the integrity standards we thought were givens. Hopeful realism is needed to bring in light to see the way forward. Leaders must find and understand the facts—the truth—understand how the situation is likely to change for the better and for the worse.

"Going over and over one's fear is empty and emptying. Something greater that sustains: I call it esperanza—hope. We [say] querer es podar. Desire is power. Hope and desire are power." [16]

~ CLARISSA PINKOLA ESTÉS, PH. D. ~
The Dangerous Old Woman

Can we hope again? Dream again? Be inspired again? Inspire others again? We must! I know the potential exists in each person on this earth to lead with hope, working to build a better tomorrow.

Never doubt that you are powerful. You can make a difference. Just as there is the potential for each acorn on the ground to grow into a mighty oak tree, you also can grow into a more inspiring leader who makes a positive difference.

"If you think you are too small to make a difference, you haven't spent the night with a mosquito." [17]

~ AFRICAN PROVERB ~

Here are a few thought starters as you lead others to reimagine their dreams and make a positive difference.

1. Create a collective understanding—The Why? Speak the facts—simple-specific and the unvarnished truth.

2. Speak from your heart. Create the narrative by telling a truly inspiring story of your own.

3. Engage others in defining the dream. Tell me what I as a specific individual can do to help achieve the dream.

4. Change your actions and your communications as the dream evolves. Each part of the journey requires a leader to grow and change along the rocky road to the "promised land."

5. Have your team of leaders sing from the same page but in their own keys. Just mouthing the same words does not inspire confidence.

6. Learn to lead as effectively through a camera lens as in person. There is no escape from using social media tools to communicate anymore.

7. Develop others as inspiring leaders and lead through others. Grow champions of the dream and make them a dream team.

8. Get your hands dirty by "doing the work" with lots of "mud on your shoes." Being shoulder-to-shoulder with your team builds commitment and is energizing.

9. Accept setbacks and detours as part of the journey. Transformational change is messy and filled with many surprises.

10. Be the chronic student who sees learning opportunities in every situation. Saying "I don't know" sparks curiosity and creativity.

11. Celebrate, congratulate, and express sincere, specific gratitude. Your job as an inspiring leader is to keep hope alive even when the lights go out.

12. Harness your team's energy, because achieving a dream requires massive amounts of everyone's energy. Keep the light in your heart shining bright to energize others.

13. Bring joy, laughter and the strength of mighty oak trees with you on every step of the journey. Stay grateful, rooted in integrity for each challenge and success.

"Never doubt that a small group of thoughtful, committed citizens can change the world: indeed, it's the only thing that ever has." [18]

~ MARGARET MEAD ~

Dreams Become Realities

Turning dreams into reality is the ultimate leadership effectiveness measure. Githesh Ramamurthy, Chairman and CEO of CCCIS explains:

". . . when I think about the Real Deal—to me, the definition of a leader is someone—because of this person—a country, an organization, a tribe, having seen all versions of those in the places that I have lived . . . this country, this tribe, this organization, this school—whatever this person is involved in as a leader . . . are they in a different, better place because of this leader or not? To me just having passion and authenticity is not the (entire) real deal—the real deal means you have the ability to affect (positive) change. Have you moved your tribe, your organization, your company to a very different place because of your leadership?"[19]

My hope for you, as you are *Being the Real Deal*, is that you lead an inspired and inspiring group of people to make our world better. We need all of us to join together to turn the dreams of freedom and equality for all into a reality. As the title of Van Gordon Martin's (my son's) first solo album reminds us, there is "No Limit to Love."[20] https://www.vangordonmartin.com

When faced with the rawest, hardest attacks, my hope for you is that you stand tall like the mighty oak tree rooted in your integrity. Most of all, I hope you "love your way through" all the challenges and opportunities you will face as an inspired and inspiring leader who is always *Being the Real Deal*.

"I have decided to stick with love. Hate is too great a burden to bear." [21]

~ DR. MARTIN LUTHER KING, JR. ~

Keep Growing!

1. How are you cultivating hope-filled environments?

2. What actions are you taking to inspire others to . . .

    - Dream More?

    - Learn More?

    - Do More?

    - Become More?

3. What will be your legacy as a leader?

"Not making a difference is a cost we cannot afford. The cause of equal and human rights will reap what is sown . . . What will you reap? What will you sow?" [22]

~ CONGRESSWOMAN BARBARA JORDAN ~
Opening Keynote Address, 1st National Women's Conference, November 18, 1977

As I listened to Congresswoman Barbara Jordan deliver the Keynote Address at the 1st National Women's Conference in 1977, I was inspired by her call to action. Two years later, I was one of 10 students in her 1st graduate seminar at the LBJ School of Public Affairs at the University of Texas at Austin upon her retirement from Congress.

Sitting next to her each week while she grilled us, I experienced one-on-one a legendary powerful, and inspiring leader. I earned an A in her class which I cherish along with this personal note. Congresswoman Barbara Jordan's challenge to make a difference in the cause of equal and human rights is at the heart of *Being the Real Deal.*

Endnotes

1. *Could have been a scene out of a television series...* Silverman, B., Daniels, G., Gervais, R., Merchant, S., Klein, H., Kwapis, K., Lieberstein, P., Celotta, J. Novak, B. J., Kaling, M., Forrester, B, Sterling, D. (Executive Producers). (2003-2015). *The Office* [TV series]. National Broadcasting Company.

2. *Could have been a scene out of a television series...* David, L., Shapiro, G., West, H., Scheinman, A., Seinfeld, J., Berg, A., Schaffer, J. (Executive Producers). (1990-1998). *Seinfeld* [TV series]. National Broadcasting Company.

3. *Leadership standards have fallen...* Neal, S., Rhyne, R. Boatman, J. Watt, B. & Yeh, M. (2023, February 8). *DDI global leadership forecast 2023*. DDI. https://www.ddiworld.com/glf.

4. *We are losing faith in our leaders...* Leaver, S. (2022, October 27). *Trust will be critical for leaders in 2023*. Forbes. https://www.forbes.com/sites/forrester/2022/10/27/trust-will-be-critical-for-leaders-in-2023/.

5. *Each chapter begins with an original illustration...* Jay, M. (2023). Original artwork designed by Missi Jay DBA Giggle Box Designs. Copyright by Dr. Vicky Gordon, The Gordon Group, Inc. No aspect of the artwork and layout may be used without written consent.

6. *Oak trees symbolize...* Mast Producing Trees (2022, September 29). *The spirit of oak tree: A source of strength comfort and inspiration.* Mast Producing Trees. https://mast-producing-trees .org/the-spirit-of-oak-tree-a-source-of-strength-comfort -and-inspiration/.

7. *Until the COVID-19 pandemic made real-time heroes...* Wilton, D. (2020, December 30). *Hero.* Wordorigins.org. https:// www.wordorigins.org/big-list-entries/hero. Note: The English word "hero" is gender neutral.

Chapter One: Leading With Mud on Your Shoes

1. *Your visible values are...* Lake Forest MBA. (2009, July 1). *ITW Chairman/CEO David Speer delivers 09 Lake Forest MBA commencement address* [Video]. YouTube. https://www .youtube.com/watch?v=WjAz8sTJ9ys

2. *Example is not the main thing...* Byers, J. (November 1995). Forward. In J, Byers. (Ed.) *Brothers in spirit: The correspondence of Albert Schweitzer and William Larimer Mellon, Jr.* (p. xviii [Forward]). Syracuse University Press.

3. *David began his ITW career...* Delgado, J. (2012, November 19). ITW Chairman and CEO David B. Speer dead at 61. *Chicago Tribune.* https://www.chicagotribune.com/business /ct-xpm-2012-11-19-chi-david-speer-itw-20121118-story.html

4. *I think you've got to reach out...* Gordon, V. (2008, March 25). *Interview with David B. Speer (Chairman, CEO of Illinois Tool Works, Inc.) on leadership challenges facing the next generations of CEOs.* [Interview]. The Gordon Group, Inc. Archives.

5. *During his years as CEO...* Strahler, S. (2012, November 18). ITW chief Speer has died; drove firm's overseas expansion. *Crain's Chicago Business.* https://www.chicagobusiness.com

/article/20121118/NEWS05/121119787/illinois-tool-works
-ceo-speer-has-died-drove-firm-s-overseas-expansion

6. *ITW had over 875 decentralized business units...* Illinois Tool
Works, Inc. (2009). *2008 annual report* (p.2). Retrieved
from: https://www.annualreports.com/HostedData
/AnnualReportArchive/i/NYSE_ITW_2008.pdf

7. *A tree can only be as strong...* Wohlleben, P. (2016). *The hidden
life of trees: What they feel, how they communicate—Discoveries
from a secret world* (Vol. 1, p. 17). Greystone Books.

8. *Decentralization is a core attribute of ITW...* Illinois Tool
Works, Inc. (2010). *2009 annual report* (p.5). Retrieved
from: https://www.annualreports.com/HostedData
/AnnualReportArchive/i/NYSE_ITW_2009.pdf

9. *ITW's proprietary 80/20 business process...* Illinois Tool Works,
Inc. (2023, n.d.). *About ITW.* ITW. https://www.itw.com
/about-itw/itw-business-model/

10. *Consistently recognized as a leading product innovator...* Illinois
Tool Works, Inc. (n.d.). *Company – ITW.* ITW Safety. http://
www.itw-deltar.com/company.php

11. *In our environment, we talk openly...* Gordon, V. (2008,
March 25). *Interview with David B. Speer (Chairman, CEO
of Illinois Tool Works, Inc.) on leadership challenges facing the
next generations of CEOs.* [Interview]. The Gordon Group,
Inc. Archives.

12. *Lehman Brothers went under...* Sraders, A. (2018, September
12). *The Lehman brothers collapse and how it's changed the
economy today.* The Street. https://www.thestreet.com
/markets/lehman-brothers-collapse-14703153

13. *The Federal Reserve and the U.S. Treasury...* Bekman, K.
(2010, February 16). *What caused the financial crisis and
recession?* Inside Edge. https://www.conferenceboard.ca

/insideedge/2010/february-2010/feb16-what-caused-the
.aspx?AspxAutoDetectCookieSupport=1

14. *U.S. labor market lost 8.4 million jobs...* Cunningham, E. (2018, April). *Great recession, great recovery? Trends from the current population survey.* U.S. Bureau of Labor Statistics. https://www.bls.gov/opub/mlr/2018/article/great-recession-great-recovery.htm

15. *David had a steady hand at the helm...* Gordon, V. (2015, November 15). *Interview with Susan Brady (retired SVP Human Resources, Illinois Tool Works, Inc.) on leadership strategy during the 2008-2009 recession* [Interview]. The Gordon Group, Inc. Archives.

16. *Quite simply the real deal...* Gordon, V. (2011, March 5). *360 Feedback interview with Susan Crown (Illinois Tool Works, Inc Board of Directors member) re David Speer (Chairman and CEO of Illinois Tool Works, Inc).* [Interview]. The Gordon Group, Inc., Inc. Archives. Note: Susan Crown is also currently Chairman & Founder at SCE.

17. *The right thing, in the right way...* Gordon, V. (2014, March 5). *Interview with Susan Crown (Illinois Tool Works, Inc Board of Directors Member) on what it means to be the real deal as a leader.* [Interview]. The Gordon Group, Inc., Inc. Archives. Note: Susan Crown is also currently Chairman & Founder at SCE.

18. *If you can remember only one message...* Lake Forest MBA. (2009, July 1). *ITW Chairman/CEO David Speer delivers 09 Lake Forest MBA commencement address* [Video]. YouTube. https://www.youtube.com/watch?v=WjAz8sTJ9ys

19. *Try not to become a man(person) of success...* Miller, W. (1955, May). Death of a genius: His fourth dimension, time, overtakes Einstein. *Time, 38*(18), p.64.

20. *Character is like a tree...* Epstein, D. M. (2008, p. 3). *The Lincolns: Portrait of a marriage.* Ballantine Books.

Chapter Two: Everyone Has a Story

1. *Every great oak...* Popik, B. (2013, February 4). *Entry from February 04, 2013.* The big apple. https://www.barrypopik .com/index.php/new_york_city/entry/every_great_oak_was _once_a_little_nut_that_held_its_ground

2. *Your invisible resume...* Gordon, V. (2009, September 8). Rewrite your invisible resume. *Harvard Business Review.* https://hbr.org/2009/09/rewrite-your-invisible-resume

3. *You put everything you've got into...* Gordon, V. (2014, March 4). *Interview with Susan Crown (Illinois Tool Works, Inc. Board of Directors member) on what it means to be the real deal as a leader.* [Interview]. The Gordon Group, Inc. Archives. Note: Susan Crown is currently Chairman & Founder at SCE.

4. *If you have done this for the least of them...* King James Bible Online (2023, n.d.). *Matthew chapter 25.* King James Bible online. https://www.kingjamesbibleonline.org/Matthew -Chapter-25/#40

5. *I do not want to go to anyone's house...* Quinion, M. (2011, February 19). *Saucered and blowed.* World wide words: Investigating the English language across the globe. https:// www.worldwidewords.org/qa/qa-sau1.htm. Note: "Saucering your coffee" is the act of pouring coffee into a saucer, thereby allowing it to cool before drinking. The expression was used predominantly in Southern and Western America beginning the 1800s.

6. *There is no greater agony... Quote attributed to Maya Angelou.* Gur, T. (2023, n.d.). *There is no greater agony than bearing an untold story inside you.* Elevate society. https://elevatesociety. com/there-is-no-greater-agony/

7. *The light that you see by...* Roch, L. (2014). *The radiance sutras: 112 gateways to the yoga of wonder and delight* (p. 72). Sounds True Publishing.

8. *Don't allow anybody to...* Beacon Press (2015, May 19). *Martin Luther King, Jr., "What Is Your Life's Blueprint?"* [Video]. YouTube. https://www.youtube.com/watch?v=ZmtOGXreTOU&t=7s.

9. *We have two things in common...* Angelou, M. (1969). *I know why the caged bird sings.* Random House, Inc.

10. *My journey to being...* Brown, B. (2019). *Dare to lead: Brave work, tough conversations, whole hearts* (pp. 72–73). Random House, Inc.

11. *I'm good enough...* Franken, A., & Beattie, M. (1992). *I'm good enough, I'm smart enough, and doggone it, people like me! Daily affirmations by Stuart Smalley.* Dell.

12. *The privilege of a lifetime...* Campbell, J., & Osbon, D. K. (1998). *A Joseph Campbell companion: Reflections on the art of living.* HarperPerennial.

13. *Even when it's not pretty...* Obama, M. (2018). *Becoming* (p. Vxii [forward]). Crown Publishing Group.

Chapter Three: Either You Have It or You Don't

1. *An oak tree's taproot...* Mast Producing Trees (2022, September 11). *The deepest taproot: An oak tree's journey.* Mast Producing Trees. https://mast-producing-trees.org/the-deepest-tap-root-an-oak-trees-journey/

2. *West Point Cadet Code of Honor...* West Point United States Military Academy (2023, n.d.). *West Point cadet honor code and honor system.* West Point United States

Military Academy. https://www.westpoint.edu/military /simon-center-for-the-professional-military-ethic/honor

3. *When we show up fully...* David, S. (2016). *Emotional agility: Get unstuck, embrace change, and thrive in work and life* (p.67). Penguin.

4. *The truth will set you free...* Steinem, G. (2019). *The truth will set you free, but first it will piss you off! Thoughts on life, love, and rebellion.* Random House.

5. *Integrity is your destiny...* quote attributed to Heraclitus (c. 540–c. 480 BC). Greek Philosopher and Cosmologist. Heraclitus > quotes. (2023, n.d.). Goodreads, Inc. https:// www.goodreads.com/author/quotes/77989.

6. *Only people who don't do anything...* O. R. Gordon, personal communications, n.d., 1914-1977.

7. *Humility is not thinking...* Warren, R. (2006). *The Purpose Driven Life* (p. 265). Findaway World.

8. *No legacy is so rich...* George Mason University (2023, n.d.). *All's well that ends well.* Open source Shakespeare. https:// www.opensourceshakespeare.org/views/plays/play_view .php?WorkID=allswell&Act=3&Scene=5&Scope=scene.

9. *Integrity is number one...* Gordon, V. (2008, March 21). *Interview with Stephen Zelnak (CEO & Chairman of Martin Marietta) on what it means to be the real deal as a leader.* [Interview]. The Gordon Group, Inc. Archives.

10. *If you sacrifice your principles...* Gordon, V. (2008, June 10). *Interview with James Sinegal, Jr. (cofounder and former CEO of Costco) on what it means to be the real deal as a leader.* [Interview]. The Gordon Group, Inc. Archives.

11. *I had gone as far as I could go...* Klammon, C (1986, September 21). Do business women have to act like men in

order to get ahead? *Chicago Tribune.* https://www.chicago tribune.com/news/ct-xpm-1986-09-21-8603100484-story.html

12. *Make lying bad again...* Reid, J. (2023, Jan n.d.). The ReidOut. MSNBC.

13. *Integrity is an all-or-nothing...* Goldsmith, M., & Reiter, M. (2015, p. 215). *Triggers: Creating behavior that lasts—becoming the person you want to be.* Currency.

14. *The Big Lie...* Yang, J. & Kahn, S (2022, April 26). How powerful conservatives pushed the "Big Lie" that the 2020 election was fraudulent. PBS News Hour. https://www .pbs.org/newshour/show/how-powerful-conservatives -pushed-the-big-lie-that-the-2020-election-was-fraudulent

15. *The danger of "The Big Lie"...* Block, M (2021, December 23). *The clear and present danger of Trump's enduring "Big Lie."* NPR. https://www.npr.org/2021/12/23/1065277246 /trump-big-lie-jan-6-election.

16. *The truth is the 2020 presidential election...* Reuters staff (2021, February 15). *Fact check: courts have dismissed multiple lawsuits of alleged electoral fraud presented by Trump campaign.* Reuters. https://www.reuters.com/article/uk-factcheck-courts -election/fact-check-courts-have-dismissed-multiple-lawsuits -of-alleged-electoral-fraud-presented-by-trump-campaign -idUSKBN2AF1G1

17. *Make lying bad again...* Reid, J. (2023, Jan n.d.). The ReidOut. MSNBC.

18. *There is truth and there are lies...* Biden, J (2021, January 20). *Inaugural address by President Joseph R. Biden, Jr.* The White House. https://www.whitehouse.gov /briefing-room/speeches-remarks/2021/01/20/inaugural -address-by-president-joseph-r-biden-jr.

19. *For there is always light...* Armenti, P. (2021, January 21). *"For there is always light": Amanda Gorman's inaugural*

poem *"The Hill We Climb" delivers message of unity.* Library of congress blogs. https://blogs.loc.gov/catbird/2021/01 /for-there-is-always-light-amanda-gormans-inaugural-poem -the-hill-we-climb-delivers-message-of-unity/

Chapter Four: The Heart of the Matter

1. *Heartwood is the central...* Daily, G. C., & Katz, C. J. (2012). *The Power of Trees* (p. 30). Trinity University Press.

2. *"Aspire Higher" slogan...* Saint Mary-of-the-Woods College (2023, n.d.). *Welcome to the woods* (p.1). Saint Mary-of-the -Woods College. https://www.smwc.edu/

3. *Work is love...* Gibran, K. (1972). *The Prophet* (p.13). Alfred A. Knopf.

4. *Your head needs to be in the game...* King, B. J (2016, February 11) *Overcoming adversity: Bringing all of yourself to everything you do.* Chicago, IL.

5. *To do something with soul...* Moore, C. (2004). *In other words: A language lover's guide to the most intriguing words around the world* (p. 103). Bloomsbury Publishing USA.

6. *The Greek word Meraki...* meraki. NPR (2005, January 19). *Translating the Untranslatable.* NPR. https://www.npr .org/2005/01/19/4457805/translating-the-untranslatable

7. *In research published in...* Sull, D., Sull, C., & Zweig (2022, January 11). *Toxic Culture Is Driving the Great Resignation.* MIT Sloan Management Review. https:// sloanreview.mit.edu/article/toxic-culture-is-driving-the-great -resignation/.

8. *I've learned that people...* Angelou, M. [@cmgworldwide and @drmyaangelou]. (2023, July 16). *I've learned that people will forget what you said, people will forget what you did, but*

people will never forget [Reel]. Instagram. https://instagram
.com/drmayaangelou?igshid=MzRlODBiNWFlZA==

9. *I would like to be known...* Angelou, M. (2014, May 28). *Obsessed: 16 Unforgettable Things Maya Angelou Wrote and Said* Glamour. https://www.glamour.com/story/maya-angelou-quotes

10. *Some people feel the rain...* Searing, B. (2019, May 14). *Some People Feel the Rain. Others Just Get Wet.* Medium. https://medium.com/@bryansearing/some-people-feel-the-rain-others-just-get-wet-b42360ff85cc

11. *And it transcends generations...* Gordon, V (2008, May 5) Interview with William Green (Chairman, CEO of Accenture) on leadership challenges facing the next generation of CEOs [Interview] The Gordon Group, Inc. Archives.

12. *Great leaders elicit passion . . .* Jones, D. (2003, October 27). *Music director works to blend strengths How to motivate staff without utilizing fear.* USA Today

13. *Great dancers are not great...* Cimon-Paquet, C. (2021, February 16). *Reflecting on our passions to change our life: Positive psychology concepts series.* Medium. https://cppastudents.medium.com/reflecting-on-our-passions-to-change-our-life-positive-psychology-concepts-series-893aa7381fdd.

14. *It is first and foremost about passion...* Gordon, V. (2014, May 29). *Interview with Githesh Ramamurthy (CEO and Chairman, CCC Intelligent Solutions) on what it means to be the real deal as a leader.* [Interview]. The Gordon Group, Inc. Archives.

15. *To play a wrong note is insignificant...* Wegeler, F. (1987). *Beethoven remembered: The biographical notes of Franz Wegeler and Ferdinand Ries* (p.94), trans. F. Noonan. Great Ocean Publishers.

16. *Nonprofits don't have a monopoly on meaning...* McGovern, G. (2014, March). Lead from the heart. *Harvard Business Review.* https://hbr.org/2014/03/lead-from-the-heart

17. *Leaders touch a heart...* Maxwell, J. C. (2007). *The 21 irrefutable laws of leadership: Follow them and people will follow you.* (p.4) HarperCollins Leadership.

18. *We saw slaves shooting...* The Associated Press (2022, March 21). Live updates: Zelenskyy says Ukraine ready to discuss deal *Ap.* https://apnews.com/article/russia-ukraine-kyiv -boris-johnson-business-europe-4b0fee549843a0a6ed73c3 14f8c2fa12

19. *We shall overcome...* Tindley, C. A. (1900). I'll Overcome Some Day [Recorded by P Seeger].

20. *Leadership is about empathy...* Blaschka, A (2019, February 19). The soft skill Gary Vaynerchuk, Simon Sinek and Oprah Winfrey say is crucial for leaders. *Forbes.* https://www .forbes.com/sites/amyblaschka/2019/02/19/the-soft-skill-gary -vaynerchuk-simon-sinek-and-oprah-winfrey-say-is-crucial -for-leaders/?sh=200d1c094e9b

Chapter Five: Paying the Price

1. *I can see in the acorn...* Douglas, A. A. (2019). *928 Maya Angelou Quotes* (Vol. 5, p. 53). UB Tech.

2. *You put your whole self in...* Ray Anthony and His Orchestra. (1953). The hokey pokey [Song]. On *The hokey pokey.* Capital Records, Inc.

3. *Behavior number one is the willingness...* Gordon, V. (2014, May 29). *Interview with Githesh Ramamurthy (CEO and Chairman, CCC Intelligent Solutions) on what it means to*

be the real deal as a leader. [Interview]. The Gordon Group, Inc. Archives.

4. *Courage is not the absence of fear...* David, S. [@SusanDavid _PhD]. (2021, February 3). *Courage is not the absence of fear. Courage is fear walking* [Tweet]. Twitter. https://twitter.com /SusanDavid_PhD/status/1356755119828848641

5. *David and Goliath matchup...* King James Bible Online (2023, n.d.). *Samuel 1 chapter 17.* King James Bible online. https:// www.kingjamesbibleonline.org/1-Samuel-Chapter-17/

6. *I need ammunition, not a ride...* Braithwaite, S. (2022, February 26). Zelensky refuses US offer to evacuate, saying *"I need ammunition, not a ride."* CNN. https://www.cnn .com/2022/02/26/europe/ukraine-zelensky-evacuation-intl /index.html

7. *At the heart of daring leadership...* Brown, B. (2018). *Dare to Lead: Brave work. Tough conversations* (p.10). *Whole hearts.* Random House.

8. *My Aunt Wilma ran a preschool...* Bennis, W., Schroeder, P., Mitchell, S. G., & Gordon, V. (2007). Interview with Dr. Vicky Gordon one of America's top leadership experts. *In leadership, helping others succeed: In-depth interviews with America's top leadership experts.* Insight Publishing.

9. *The more slowly trees grow...* Thoreau, H. D. (1892). *Autumn: From the journey of Henry David Throeau* (pp. 385–462). (H. G. O. Blake, Ed.). Houghton Mifflin and Company.

10. *Always take your clients where they are…* Gallessich, J. (1982). *The profession and practice of consultation: Handbook for consultants, trainers of consultants and consumer of consultation services.* Jossey-Bass Social and Behavioral Science Series. Note: Dr. June Gallessich was my mentor, served on my dissertation committee at the University of Texas at Austin, and taught me how to be an effective and value-based change

agent. Dr. Gallessich is one of the ongoing inspirations of my professional and personal life. I am forever grateful for her caring mentorship, friendship, and her gifts of wisdom to me.

11. *Between stimulus and response...* Frankl, V. E. (1984). *Man's search for meaning: An introduction to logotherapy.* Simon and Schuster. Frankl speaks to this approach in his book, but did not write these exact words. The author is unknown.

12. *In 2021, white supremacists...* Tucker, E. (2021, March 2). FBI chief warns violent "domestic terrorism" growing in US. *The Associated Press.* https://apnews.com/article/fbi-chris-wray-testify-capitol-riot-9a5539af34b15338bb5c492 3907eeb67

13. *If you can only be tall because...* Rose, C. (1993, May 7). Novelist Toni Morrison looks back on her youth and family and presents her newest book, "Jazz." [Video]. *Charile Rose.* https://charlierose.com/videos/18778

14. *She was the only known white...* Phang, K. (2023, March 5). *The Story of Civil Rights Activist Viola Liuzzo.* MSNBC. https://www.msnbc.com/katie-phang/watch/the-story-of-civil-rights-activist-viola-liuzzo-164508229885

15. *It's everyone's fight...* Phang, K. (2023, March 5). *The Story of Civil Rights Activist Viola Liuzzo.* MSNBC. https://www.msnbc.com/katie-phang/watch/the-story-of-civil-rights-activist-viola-liuzzo-164508229885

16. *I truly believe this is a moment...* Klobuchar, A. [@MSNBC]. (2020, June 18). *Klobuchar: Joe Biden Should Pick a Woman of Color as VP* [Tweet] Twitter. https://twitter.com/MSNBC/status/1273803046687047681?ref_src=twsrc%5Etfw%7Ctwcamp%5Etweetembed%7Ctwterm%5E1273803046687047681%7Ctwgr%5E795aeb3ab1b5ad854bc673da4c3d9b7e7f020c5b%7Ctwcon%5Es1_&ref_url=https%3A%2F%2

Fwww.npr.org%2F2020%2F06%2F18%2F880706319%2Fklobuchar-withdraws-from-vp-consideration-says-biden-should-pick-a-woman-of-color

17. *I may be the first woman...* Harris, K. [@kamalaharris]. (2020 November 7.). *While I may be the first woman in this office, I will not be the last* [Tweet]. Twitter. https://twitter.com/KamalaHarris/status/13252510505509639681

18. *Anyone who claims to be a leader...* Harris, K. [@kamalaharris]. (2019, January 28.). *Anyone who claims to be a leader must speak like a leader. That means speaking with integrity and truth* [Tweet]. Twitter. https://www.instagram.com/p/BtNCOpGjx41/

Chapter Six: Endings and Beginnings

1. *The axe forgets...* Spice FM (2021, June 4). Today's proverb: *The axe forgets, the tree remembers*—(African Proverb)#TheSituationRoom Eric Latiff .@nduokoh CT Muga .@ktnhome_[Video]. Facebook. https://www.facebook.com/watch/?v=326402759060590

2. *Much has been written about...* Blount, S. (2018, February 12). Leaving well: Why the last 90 days matter. *Forbes.* https://www.forbes.com/sites/sallyblount/2018/02/12/leaving-well-why-the-last-90-days-matters-more-than-the-first-90/?sh=1f9b597d6d7e

3. *Execution eats strategy...* Gordon, V. (2008, June 11). *Interview with Jim Skinner (Non-Executive Director, Walgreens Boots Alliance, Inc. and retired CEO of McDonald's) on the challenges facing the next generation of CEOs.* [Interview]. The Gordon Group, Inc. Archives.

4. *A bad system will beat...* Deming, W. E. (1993, n. d.). Deming Four Day Seminar. [Lecture Notes]. https://deming.org/a-bad-system-will-beat-a-good-person-every-time/

5. *Crossed the rubicon...* Rosengren, A. (n.d.). *Iacta alea est: Crossing the rubicon.* Latinitium. https://latinitium.com/iacta-alea-est-crossing-the-rubicon/#:~:text=On%20January%2010th%2C%2049%20B.C.,Roman%20Civil%20War%

6. *Talent, just pure talent...* Gordon, V. (2008, April 14). *Interview with Robert Lane (then Chairman and CEO of Deere & Company) on the challenges facing the next generation of CEOs.* [Interview]. The Gordon Group, Inc. Archives.

7. *Despite its importance...* Blount, S. (2018, February 12). Leaving well: Why the last 90 days matter. *Forbes.* https://www.forbes.com/sites/sallyblount/2018/02/12/leaving-well-why-the-last-90-days-matters-more-than-the-first-90/?sh=1f9b597d6d7e

8. *The problem in many organizations...* Gordon, V. (2014, May 29). *Interview with Githesh Ramamurthy (CEO and Chairman, CCC Intelligent Solutions) on what it means to be the real deal as a leader.* [Interview]. The Gordon Group, Inc. Archives.

9. *Nothing is a success until...* Gordon, V. (2008, June 11). *Interview with Jim Skinner (Non-Executive Director, Walgreens Boots Alliance, Inc. and retired CEO of McDonald's) on the challenges facing the next generation of CEOs.* [Interview]. The Gordon Group, Inc. Archives.

10. *"James," Global CIO...* This chapter was written in collaboration with my client called James, which is not the person's name. First names and other personal attributes have been modified to protect individuals' identities in this and other chapters. Any likeness to others is accidental.

Chapter Seven: Chronic Student

1. *You see, the tough part is...* Gordon, V. (personal communication, n.d.)

2. *I have no special talent...* Einstein, A. (personal communication, March 11, 1952). https://libquotes.com/albert-einstein/quote/lbu7b9p

3. The cure for boredom... Parr E. Quotable Quotes, 1980 December, Reader's Digest, Vol. 117. Quotable Quotes, Quote Page 172, The Reader's Digest Association. www.quoteinvestigator.com

4. *Whatever inspiration is...* Szymborska, W. (1996, December 7). *The Poet and the world. [Nobel lecture].* The Nobel prize in literature 1996. Stockholm, Sweden. https://www.nobelprize.org/prizes/literature/1996/szymborska/lecture/

5. *Take Michaelangelo for example...* Dewy, R. A. (2020, October 1). *The magic spell is ancora imparo. Medium.* https://medium.com/@rachmianindya/the-magic-spell-is-ancora-imparo-d1e7bccb8270

6. *The legendary cellist...* Graham, T (2007, January 5). After the gifts are opened, what's next?" *Herald Democrat*, Section: Religion.

7. *Then there is the 95-year-old...* Huston-Crespo, m. (2022, November 17). *Angela Álvarez makes history at age 95 with Latin Grammy tie win for best new artist.* CNN entertainment. https://www.cnn.com/2022/11/17/entertainment/angela-alvarez-best-new-artist-latin-grammys/index.html

8. *Susan Crown, Chairman and Founder at SCE advises...* Gordon, V. (2014, March 5). *Interview with Susan Crown (Illinois Tool Works, Inc Board of Directors member) on what it means to be the real deal as a leader.* [Interview]. The Gordon Group, Inc.

Archives. Note: Susan Crown is currently Chairman & Founder at SCE.

9. *Listen, learn, then lead...* Gordon, V. (2008, August 25). *Interview with Greg Brown (Chairman and Chief Executive Officer of Motorola Solutions, Inc.) on the challenges facing the next generation of CEOs.* [Interview]. The Gordon Group, Inc. Archives.

10. Knowles, B. (n.d.). *Beyonce Knowles Quotes.* BrainyQuote. https://www.brainyquote.com/quotes/beyonce_knowles_596349

Chapter Eight: Everyone Has a Dream

1. *If your actions create a legacy...* attributed to Dolly Parton. Adrian, L. A. (Ed.). (1997). *The most important thing I Know: life lessons from Colin Powell, Stephen Covey, Maya Angelou and over 75 other eminent individuals* (pp. 60-61). Cader/Andrews and McMeel.

2. *Dream more, learn more, do more...* attributed to Dolly Parton. Adrian, L. A. (Ed.). (1997). *The most important thing I know: life lessons from Colin Powell, Stephen Covey, Maya Angelou and over 75 other eminent individuals* (pp. 60-61). Cader/Andrews and McMeel.

3. *As we gather more years...* Estés, C. P. (1996). *The dangerous old woman: Myths and stories of the wild woman archetype* (C.P. Estés, Narr.) [Audiobook]. Sounds True. https://www.soundstrue.com/products/the-dangerous-old-woman

4. *We seem unwilling to use our best qualities...* Bennis, W. (1989). *Why leaders can't lead* (pp. 118-120). San Francisco: Jossey-Bass.

5. *Boldly go where no man has gone before...* Oxford University Press (n.d.) *Oxford reference: boldly go where no man has gone before*

[TV]. https://www.oxfordreference.com/display/10.1093/acref/9780199567454.001.0001/acref-9780199567454-e-274

6. *It takes a village...* Clinton, H. R. (1996). *It takes a village and other lessons children teach us.* Simon & Schuster.

7. *Not everybody can be famous...* Karmatube (2016, n. d.). *Everybody Can Be Great, Martin Luther King, Jr.* [Video]. KarmaTube. https://www.karmatube.org/videos.php?id=2959#:~:text=Debug%20log-,Everybody%20Can%20Be%20Great%2C%20Martin%20Luther%20King%2C%20Jr.,%2C%20Martin%20Luther%20King%2C%20Jr.

8. *I have been to the mountaintop...* NPR (2023, Jan 16). *Read Martin Luther King Jr.'s "'I Have a Dream" speech in its entirety.* NPR. https://www.npr.org/2010/01/18/122701268/i-have-a-dream-speech-in-its-entirety

9. *I find that people want to do challenging...* Gordon, V. (2008, May 5). *Interview with William Green (President CEO Accenture) on leadership challenges facing the next generations of CEOs.* [Interview]. The Gordon Group, Inc. Archives.

10. *Acorns need the right soil conditions...* Graham, A (2018, August 17). *The life cycle of an acorn seedling into a tree.* Sciencing. https://sciencing.com/the-life-cycle-of-an-acorn-seedling-into-a-tree-12486565.html

11. *The definition of responsible...* Douglas Harper (n.d.). *responsible (adj.).* Online etymology dictionary. https://www.etymonline.com/word/responsible

12. *Dream more, learn more, do more... attributed to Dolly Parton.* Adrian, L. A. (Ed.). (1997). *The most important thing I know: life lessons from Colin Powell, Stephen Covey, Maya Angelou and over 75 other eminent individuals* (pp. 60-61). Cader/Andrews and McMeel.

13. *Hope is the thing with feathers...* Academy of American Poets (n.d.) *Hope is the thing with feathers* (254). Poets.org. https://poets.org/poem/hope-thing-feathers-254

14. *What happens to a dream deferred...* Hughes, L. (1902-1967). *The collected poems of Langston Hughes.* Knopf: Distributed by Random House.

15. *The great resignation...* Helter, A & Kerner, S. M. (2023, July 3). *The great resignation: Everything you need to know.* TechTarget: https://www.techtarget.com/whatis/feature/The-Great-Resignation-Everything-you-need-to-know?Offer=abt_pubpro_AI-Insider

16. *Going over and over...* Estés, C. P. (1996). *The dangerous old woman: Myths and stories of the wild woman archetype* (C.P. Estés, Narr.) [Audiobook]. Sounds True. https://www.soundstrue.com/products/the-dangerous-old-woman

17. *If you think you are too small...* Liles, M. (2023, Feb 1). *150 of the best African proverbs about life, love and family that are full of poetic wisdom.* Parade. https://parade.com/1100530/marynliles/african-proverbs/

18. *Never doubt that a small group...* Keys,D. (1982, n.d.). *Earth at omega: Passage to planetization by Donald Keys* (p. 79). Branden Press.

19. *When I think about the Real Deal...* Gordon, V. (2014, May 29). *Interview with Githesh Ramamurthy (CEO and Chairman, CCC Intelligent Solutions) on what it means to be the real deal as a leader.* [Interview]. The Gordon Group, Inc. Archives.

20. No *Limit to Love...* Van Gordon Martin (2011, January 25). *No limit to love* [Album]. Van Gordon Martin.

21. *I have decided to stick with love... (2022, n.d.) Martin Luther King, Jr.* Quotespedia.org. https://www.quotespedia.org/authors/m/martin-luther-king-jr/i-have-decided-to-stick-with-love-hate-is-too-great-a-burden-to-bear-martin-luther-king-jr/

22. *Not making a difference...* Jordan, B. (1977, November 18). *Opening keynote address* [Keynote Speaker]. 1st National Women's Conference. Houston, TX, United States.

Bibliography

Academy of American Poets (n.d.) *Hope is the thing with feathers (254)*. Poets.org. https://poets.org/poem/hope-thing-feathers-254

Adrian, L. A. (Ed.). (1997). *The most important thing I Know: life lessons from Colin Powell, Stephen Covey, Maya Angelou and over 75 other eminent individuals* (pp. 60—61). Cader/Andrews and McMeel.

Angelou, M. (2014, May 28). *Obsessed: 16 Unforgettable Things Maya Angelou Wrote and Said* Glamour. https://www.glamour.com/story/maya-angelou-quotes

Angelou, M. (1969). *I know why the caged bird sings*. Random House, Inc.

Angelou, M. [@cmgworldwide and @drmyaangelou]. (2023, July 16). *I've learned that people will forget what you said, people will forget what you did, but people will never forget* [Reel]. Instagram. https://instagram.com/drmayaangelou?igshid=MzRlODBiNWFlZA==

Armenti, P. (2021, January 21). *"For there is always light": Amanda Gorman's inaugural poem "The Hill We Climb" delivers message of unity*. Library of congress blogs. https://blogs.loc.gov/catbird/2021/01/for-there-is-always-light-amanda-gormans-inaugural-poem-the-hill-we-climb-delivers-message-of-unity/

Beacon Press (2015, May 19). *Martin Luther King, Jr., "What Is Your Life's Blueprint?"* [Video]. YouTube. https://www.youtube.com/watch?v=ZmtOGXreTOU&t=7s.

Bekman, K. (2010, February 16). *What caused the financial crisis and recession?* Inside Edge. https://www.conferenceboard.ca/insideedge/2010/february-2010/feb16-what-caused-the.aspx?AspxAutoDetectCookieSupport=1

Bennis, W. (1989). *Why leaders can't lead (pp. 118—120).* San Francisco: Jossey-Bass.

Bennis, W. G., & Peters, T. (2000). *Managing the dream: Reflections on leadership and change.* Basic Books.

Bennis, W.,Schroeder, P., Mitchell, S. G., & Gordon, V. (2007). Interview with Dr. Vicky Gordon one of America's top leadership experts. In *leadership, helping others succeed: In-depth interviews with America's top leadership experts.* Insight Publishing.

Biden, J. (2021, January 20). *Inaugural address by President Joseph R. Biden, Jr.* The White House. https://www.whitehouse.gov/briefing-room/speeches-remarks/2021/01/20/inaugural-address-by-president-joseph-r-biden-jr.

Bird, C. (1978). The Spirit of Houston. The First National Women's Conference. An Official Report to the President, the Congress, and the People of the United States.

Blaschka, A (2019, February 19). The soft skill Gary Vaynerchuk, Simon Sinek and Oprah Winfrey say is crucial for leaders. *Forbes.* https://www.forbes.com/sites/amyblaschka/2019/02/19/the-soft-skill-gary-vaynerchuk-simon-sinek-and-oprah-winfrey-say-is-crucial-for-leaders/?sh=200d1c094e9b

Block, M (2021, December 23). *The clear and present danger of Trump's enduring "Big Lie."* NPR. https://www.npr.org/2021/12/23/1065277246/trump-big-lie-jan-6-election.

Blount, S. (2018, February 12). Leaving well: Why the last 90 days matter. *Forbes.* https://www.forbes.com/sites/sallyblount/2018/02/12/leaving-well-why-the-last-90-days-matters-more-than-the-first-90/?sh=1f9b597d6d7e

Braithwaite, S. (2022, February 26). *Zelensky refuses US offer to evacuate, saying "I need ammunition, not a ride."* CNN. https://www.cnn.com/2022/02/26/europe/ukraine-zelensky-evacuation-intl/index.html

Brown, B. (2015). *Daring greatly: How the courage to be vulnerable transforms the way we live, love, parent, and lead.* Penguin.

Brown, B. (2018). *Dare to Lead: Brave work. Tough conversations* (p.10, pp 72—73). *Whole hearts.* Random House.

Byers, J. (November 1995). Forward. In J, Byers. (Ed.) *Brothers in spirit: The correspondence of Albert Schweitzer and William Larimer Mellon, Jr.* (p. xviii [Forward]). Syracuse University Press.

Cameron, J. (1992*). The artist's way: A spiritual path to higher creativity.* Tarcher.

Cameron, J. (1999). *The right to write: An invitation and initiation into the writing life.* Penguin.

Cameron, J. (2005). *The sound of paper.* Penguin.

Campbell, J., & Osbon, D. K. (1998). *A Joseph Campbell companion: Reflections on the art of living.* HarperPerennial.

Canton, J. (2020). *The Oak Papers.* Black Inc.

Cimon-Paquet, C. (2021, February 16). *Reflecting on our passions to change our life: Positive psychology concepts series.* Medium. https://cppastudents.medium.com/reflecting-on-our-passions-to-change-our-life-positive-psychology-concepts-series-893aa7381fdd.

Clinton, H. R. (1996). *It takes a village and other lessons children teach us.* Simon & Schuster.

Cunningham, E. (2018, April). *Great recession, great recovery? Trends from the current population survey.* U.S. Bureau of Labor Statistics. https://www.bls.gov/opub/mlr/2018/article /great-recession-great-recovery.htm

Daily, G. C., & Katz, C. J. (2012). *The Power of Trees* (p. 30). Trinity University Press.

David, L., Shapiro, G., West, H., Scheinman, A., Seinfeld, J., Berg, A., Schaffer, J. (Executive Producers). (1990—1998). *Seinfeld* [TV series]. National Broadcasting Company.

David, S. (2016). *Emotional agility: Get unstuck, embrace change, and thrive in work and life (p.67)*. Penguin.

David, S. [@SusanDavid_PhD]. (2021, February 3). *Courage is not the absence of fear. Courage is fear walking* [Tweet]. Twitter. https://twitter.com/SusanDavid_PhD /status/1356755119828848641

Delgado, J. (2012, November 19). ITW Chairman and CEO David B. Speer dead at 61. *Chicago Tribune.* https://www .chicagotribune.com/business/ct-xpm-2012-11-19-chi-david -speer-itw-20121118-story.html

Deming, W. E. (1993, n. d.). Deming Four Day Seminar. [Lecture Notes]. https://deming.org/a-bad-system-will-beat -a-good-person-every-time/

Dewy, R. A. (2020, October 1). *The magic spell is ancora imparo.* Medium. https://medium.com/@rachmianindya/the-magic -spell-is-ancora-imparo-d1e7bccb8270

Douglas Harper (n.d.). *responsible (adj.).* Online etymology dictionary. https://www.etymonline.com/word/responsible

Douglas, A. A. (2019). *928 Maya Angelou Quotes* (Vol. 5, p. 53). UB Tech.

Einstein, A. (personal communication, March 11, 1952). https:// libquotes.com/albert-einstein/quote/lbu7b9p

Epstein, D. M. (2008, p. 3). *The Lincolns: Portrait of a marriage.* Ballantine Books.

Estés, C. P. (1996). *The dangerous old woman: Myths and stories of the wild woman archetype* (C.P. Estés, Narr.) [Audiobook]. Sounds True. https://www.soundstrue.com/products/the -dangerous-old-woman

Franken, A., & Beattie, M. (1992). *I'm good enough, I'm smart enough, and doggone it, people like me! Daily affirmations by Stuart Smalley.* Dell.

Frankl, V. E. (1984). *Man's search for meaning: An introduction to logotherapy.* Simon and Schuster. Frankl speaks to this approach in his book but did not write these exact words. The author is unknown.

Gallessich, J. (1982). *The profession and practice of consultation: Handbook for consultants, trainers of consultants and consumer of consultation services.* Jossey-Bass Social and Behavioral Science Series. Note: Dr. June Gallessich was my mentor, served on my dissertation committee at the University of Texas at Austin, and taught me how to be an effective and value-based change agent. Dr. Gallessich is one of the ongoing inspirations of my professional and personal life. I am forever grateful for her caring mentorship, friendship, and her gifts of wisdom to me.

George Mason University (2023, n.d.). *All's well that ends well.* Open source Shakespeare. https://www.opensourceshakespeare. org/views/plays/play_view.php?WorkID=allswell&Act=3 &Scene=5&Scope=scene.

Gibran, K. (1972). *The Prophet* (p.13). Alfred A. Knopf.

Goldsmith, M., & Reiter, M. (2015, p. 215). *Triggers: Creating behavior that lasts—becoming the person you want to be.* Currency.

Gordon, V. (2008, April 14). *Interview with Robert Lane (then Chairman and CEO of Deere & Company) on the challenges facing the next generation of CEOs.* [Interview]. The Gordon Group Archives.

Gordon, V. (2008, August 25). *Interview with Greg Brown (Chairman and Chief Executive Officer of Motorola Solutions) on the challenges facing the next generation of CEOs.* [Interview]. The Gordon Group Archives.

Gordon, V. (2008, June 10). *Interview with James Sinegal, Jr. (cofounder and former CEO of Costco) on what it means to be the real deal as a leader.* [Interview]. The Gordon Group Archives.

Gordon, V. (2008, June 11). *Interview with Jim Skinner (Non-Executive Director, Walgreens Boots Alliance, Inc. and retired CEO of McDonald's) on the challenges facing the next generation of CEOs.* [Interview]. The Gordon Group Archives.

Gordon, V. (2008, March 21). *Interview with Stephen Zelnak (CEO & Chairman of Martin Marietta) on the challenges facing the next generation of CEOs.* [Interview]. The Gordon Group Archives.

Gordon, V. (2008, March 25). *Interview with David B. Speer (Chairman, CEO of Illinois Tool Works, Inc.) on leadership challenges facing the next generations of CEOs.* [Interview]. The Gordon Group Archives.

Gordon, V. (2009, September 8). *Rewrite your invisible resume. Harvard Business Review.* https://hbr.org/2009/09/rewrite-your-invisible-resume

Gordon, V. (2011, March 5). *360 Feedback interview with Susan Crown (Illinois Tool Works, Inc Board of Directors member) re David Speer (Chairman and CEO of Illinois Tool Works, Inc).* [Interview]. The Gordon Group Archives. Note: Susan Crown is currently Chairman & Founder at SCE.

Gordon, V. (2014, March 5). *Interview with Susan Crown (Illinois Tool Works, Inc Board of Directors Member) on what it means to be the real deal as a leader.* [Interview]. The Gordon Group Archives. Note: Susan Crown is currently Chairman & Founder at SCE.

Gordon, V. (2014, May 29). *Interview with Githesh Ramamurthy (CEO and Chairman, CCC Intelligent Solutions) on what it means to be the real deal as a leader.* [Interview]. The Gordon Group Archives.

Gordon, V. (2015, November 15). *Interview with Susan Brady (retired SVP Human Resources, Illinois Tool Works, Inc.) on leadership strategy during the 2008—2009 recession* [Interview]. The Gordon Group Archives.

Gordon, V., & Martin, D. (2019). The 21st-Century CEO: Intrinsic attributes, worldview, and communication capabilities. *Journal of leadership & organizational studies, 26*(2), 141–149.

Graham, A (2018, August 17). *The life cycle of an acorn seedling into a tree.* Sciencing. https://sciencing.com/the-life-cycle-of-an-acorn-seedling-into-a-tree-12486565.html

Graham, T (2007, January 5). "After the gifts are opened, what's next?" *Herald Democrat,* Section: Religion.

Greer, C. (2014). *Change your story, change your life: Using shamanic and Jungian tools to achieve personal transformation.* Simon and Schuster.

Gur, T. (2023, n.d.). *There is no greater agony than bearing an untold story inside you.* Elevate society. https://elevatesociety.com/there-is-no-greater-agony/

Harris, K. [@kamalaharris]. (2019, January 28.). *Anyone who claims to be a leader must speak like a leader. That means speaking with integrity and truth* [Tweet]. Twitter. https://www.instagram.com/p/BtNCOpGjx41/

Harris, K. [@kamalaharris]. (2020 November 7.). *While I may be the first woman in this office, I will not be the last*

[Tweet]. Twitter. https://twitter.com/KamalaHarris/status/1325251050509639681

Haskell, D. G. (2018). *The songs of trees: Stories from nature's great connectors.* Penguin.

Helter, A & Kerner, S. M. (2023, July 3). *The great resignation: Everything you need to know.* TechTarget: https://www.techtarget.com/whatis/feature/The-Great-Resignation-Everything-you-need-to-know?Offer=abt_pubpro_AI-Insider

Heraclitus (c. 540—c. 480 BC). Greek Philosopher and Cosmologist. Heraclitus > quotes. (2023, n.d.). Goodreads, Inc. https://www.goodreads.com/author/quotes/77989.

Hughes, L. (1902—1967). *The collected poems of Langston Hughes.* Knopf: Distributed by Random House.

Huston-Crespo, m. (2022, November 17). *Angela Álvarez makes history at age 95 with Latin Grammy tie win for best new artist.* CNN entertainment. https://www.cnn.com/2022/11/17/entertainment/angela-alvarez-best-new-artist-latin-grammys/index.html

Illinois Tool Works, Inc. (2009). *2008 annual report* (p.2). Retrieved from: https://www.annualreports.com/HostedData/AnnualReportArchive/i/NYSE_ITW_2008.pdf

Illinois Tool Works, Inc. (2010). *2009 annual report* (p.5). Retrieved from: https://www.annualreports.com/HostedData/AnnualReportArchive/i/NYSE_ITW_2009.pdf

Illinois Tool Works, Inc. (2023, n.d.). *About ITW.* ITW. https://www.itw.com/about-itw/itw-business-model/

Illinois Tool Works, Inc. (n.d.). *Company—ITW.* ITW Safety. http://www.itw-deltar.com/company.php

Jay, M. (2023). Original artwork designed by Missi Jay DBA Giggle Box Designs. Copyright by Dr. Vicky Gordon, LLC.

No aspect of the artwork and layout may be used without written consent.

Jones, D. (2003, October 27). *Music director works to blend strengths How to motivate staff without utilizing fear.* USA Today.

Jordan, B. (1977, November 18). *Opening keynote address* [Keynote Speaker]. 1st National Women's Conference. Houston, TX, United States.

Karmatube (2016, n. d.). *Everybody Can Be Great, Martin Luther King, Jr.*[Video]. KarmaTube. https://www.karmatube.org/videos.php?id=2959#:~:text=Debug%20log-,Everybody%20Can%20Be%20Great%2C%20Martin%20Luther%20King%2C%20Jr.,%2C%20Martin%20Luther%20King%2C%20Jr.

Keys,D. (1982, n.d.). *Earth at omega: Passage to planetization by Donald Keys (p. 79).* Branden Press.

King James Bible Online (2023, n.d.). *Matthew chapter 25.* King James Bible online. https://www.kingjamesbibleonline.org/Matthew-Chapter-25/#40

King James Bible Online (2023, n.d.). *Samuel 1 chapter 17.* King James Bible online. https://www.kingjamesbibleonline.org/1-Samuel-Chapter-17/

King Jr., M. L. (2022, n.d.) Quotespedia.org. https://www.quotespedia.org/authors/m/martin-luther-king-jr/i-have-decided-to-stick-with-love-hate-is-too-great-a-burden-to-bear-martin-luther-king-jr/

King, B. J (2016, February 11) *Overcoming adversity: Bringing all of yourself to everything you do.* Chicago, IL.

Klammon, C (1986, September 21). Do business women have to act like men in order to get ahead? *Chicago Tribune.* https://www.chicagotribune.com/news/ct-xpm-1986-09-21-8603100484-story.html

Klobuchar, A. [@MSNBC]. (2020, June 18). *Klobuchar: Joe Biden Should Pick a Woman of Color as VP* [Tweet] Twitter. https://twitter.com/MSNBC/status/1273803046687047681?ref _src=twsrc%5Etfw%7Ctwcamp%5Etweetembed%7Ctwter m%5E1273803046687047681%7Ctwgr%5E795aeb3ab 1b5ad854bc673da4c3d9b7e7f020c5b%7Ctwcon%5Es1_&ref _url=https%3A%2F%2Fwww.npr.org%2F2020%2F06% 2F18%2F880706319%2Fklobuchar-withdraws-from-vp -consideration-says-biden-should-pick-a-woman-of-color

Knowles, B. (n.d.). *Beyonce Knowles Quotes.* BrainyQuote. https://www.brainyquote.com/quotes/beyonce_knowles_596349

Lake Forest MBA. (2009, July 1). *ITW Chairman/CEO David Speer delivers 09 Lake Forest MBA commencement address* [Video]. YouTube. https://www.youtube.com /watch?v=WjAz8sTJ9ys

Leaver, S. (2022, October 27). *Trust will be critical for leaders in 2023.* Forbes. https://www.forbes.com/sites /forrester/2022/10/27/trust-will-be-critical-for-leaders-in-2023/.

Lewis-Stempel, J. (2018). *Glorious Life of the Oak.* Doubleday.

Liles, M. (2023, Feb 1). *150 of the best African proverbs about life, love and family that are full of poetic wisdom.* Parade. https:// parade.com/1100530/marynliles/african-proverbs/

Lubar, K., & Halpern, B. L. (2004). *Leadership presence.* Penguin.

Mast Producing Trees (2022, September 11). *The deepest taproot: An oak tree's journey.* Mast Producing Trees. https://mast -producing-trees.org/the-deepest-tap-root-an-oak-trees -journey/

Mast Producing Trees (2022, September 29). *The spirit of oak tree: A source of strength comfort and inspiration.* Mast Producing Trees. https://mast-producing-trees.org/the-spirit-of-oak-tree -a-source-of-strength-comfort-and-inspiration/.

Maxwell, J. C. (2007). *The 21 irrefutable laws of leadership: Follow them and people will follow you.* (p.4) HarperCollins Leadership.

McGovern, G. (2014, March). Lead from the heart. *Harvard Business Review.* https://hbr.org/2014/03/lead-from-the-heart

Miller, W. (1955, May). Death of a genius: His fourth dimension, time, overtakes Einstein. *Time, 38*(18), p.64.

Moore, C. (2004). *In other words: A language lover's guide to the most intriguing words around the world* (p. 103). Bloomsbury Publishing USA.

Neal, S., Rhyne, R. Boatman, J. Watt, B. & Yeh, M. (2023, February 8). *DDI global leadership forecast 2023.* DDI. https://www.ddiworld.com/glf.

NPR (2005, January 19). *Translating the Untranslatable.* NPR. https://www.npr.org/2005/01/19/4457805/translating-the-untranslatable

NPR (2023, Jan 16). *Read Martin Luther King Jr.'s 'I Have a Dream' speech in its entirety.* NPR. https://www.npr.org/2010/01/18/122701268/i-have-a-dream-speech-in-its-entirety

Obama, M. (2018). *Becoming* (p. Vxii [forward]). Crown Publishing Group.

Oxford University Press (n.d.) *Oxford reference: boldly go where no man has gone before [TV].* https://www.oxfordreference.com/display/10.1093/acref/9780199567454.001.0001/acref-9780199567454-e-274

Phang, K. (2023, March 5). *The Story of Civil Rights Activist Viola Liuzzo.* MSNBC. *https://www.msnbc.com/katie-phang/watch/the-story-of-civil-rights-activist-viola-liuzzo-164508229885*

Popik, B. (2013, February 4). *Entry from February 04, 2013.* The big apple. https://www.barrypopik.com/index.php/new

_york_city/entry/every_great_oak_was_once_a_little
_nut_that_held_its_ground

Quinion, M. (2011, February 19). *Saucered and blowed*. World wide words: Investigating the English language across the globe. https://www.worldwidewords.org/qa/qa-sau1.htm. Note: "Saucering your coffee" is the act of pouring coffee into a saucer, thereby allowing it to cool before drinking. The expression was used predominantly in Southern and Western America beginning the 1800s.

Ray Anthony and His Orchestra. (1953). The hokey pokey [Song]. On *The hokey pokey*. Capital Records, Inc.

Reid, J. (2023, Jan n.d.). The ReidOut. MSNBC.

Reuters staff (2021, February 15). *Fact check: courts have dismissed multiple lawsuits of alleged electoral fraud presented by Trump campaign*. Reuters. https://www.reuters.com/article/uk-factcheck-courts-election/fact-check-courts-have-dismissed-multiple-lawsuits-of-alleged-electoral-fraud-presented-by-trump-campaign-idUSKBN2AF1G1

Roch, L. (2014). *The radiance sutras: 112 gateways to the yoga of wonder and delight* (p. 72). Sounds True Publishing.

Rose, C. (1993, May 7). Novelist Toni Morrison looks back on her youth and family and presents her newest book, "Jazz." [Video]. *Charile Rose*. https://charlierose.com/videos/18778

Rosengren, A. (n.d.). *Iacta alea est: Crossing the rubicon*. Latinitium. https://latinitium.com/iacta-alea-est-crossing-the-rubicon/#:~:text=On%20January%2010th%2C%2049%20B.C.,Roman%20Civil%20War%

Saint Mary-of-the-Woods College (2023, n.d.). Welcome *to the woods* (p.1). Saint Mary-of-the-Woods College. https://www.smwc.edu/

Searing, B. (2019, May 14). *Some People Feel the Rain. Others Just Get Wet.* Medium. https://medium.com/@bryansearing /some-people-feel-the-rain-others-just-get-wet-b42360ff85cc

Silverman, B., Daniels, G., Gervais, R., Merchant, S., Klein, H., Kwapis, K., Lieberstein, P., Celotta, J. Novak, B. J., Kaling, M., Forrester, B, Sterling, D. (Executive Producers). (2003—2015). *The Office* [TV series]. National Broadcasting Company.

Simard, S. (2021). *Finding the mother tree: Uncovering the wisdom and intelligence of the forest.* Penguin UK.

Spice FM (2021, June 4). Today's proverb: *The axe forgets, the tree remembers.—(African Proverb)#TheSituationRoom Eric Latiff .@nduokoh CT Muga .@ktnhome_*[Video]. Facebook. https://www.facebook.com/watch/?v=326402759060590

Sraders, A. (2018, September 12). *The Lehman brothers collapse and how it's changed the economy today.* The Street. https://www .thestreet.com/markets/lehman-brothers-collapse-14703153

Steinem, G. (2019). *The truth will set you free, but first it will piss you off! Thoughts on life, love, and rebellion.* Random House.

Strahler, S. (2012, November 18). ITW chief Speer has died; drove firm's overseas expansion. *Crain's Chicago Business.* https://www.chicagobusiness.com/article /20121118/NEWS05/121119787/illinois-tool-works-ceo -speer-has-died-drove-firm-s-overseas-expansion

Sull, D., Sull, C., & Zweig (2022, January 11). *Toxic Culture Is Driving the Great Resignation.* MIT Sloan Management Review. https://sloanreview.mit.edu/article/toxic-culture-is -driving-the-great-resignation/.

Szymborska, W. (1996, December 7). *The Poet and the world.* [*Nobel lecture*]. The Nobel prize in literature 1996. Stockholm, Sweden. https://www.nobelprize.org/prizes/literature/1996 /szymborska/lecture/

The Associated Press (2022, March 21). Live updates: Zelenskyy says Ukraine ready to discuss deal *Ap*. https://apnews.com/article /russia-ukraine-kyiv-boris-johnson-business-europe-4b0fee 549843a0a6ed73c314f8c2fa12

Thoreau, H. D. (1892). *Autumn: From the journey of Henry David Throeau* (pp. 385—462). (H. G. O. Blake, Ed.). Houghton Mifflin and Company.

Tindley, C. A. (1900). I'll Overcome Some Day [Recorded by P Seeger].

Tucker, E. (2021, March 2). FBI chief warns violent "domestic terrorism" growing in US. *The Associated Press.* https:// apnews.com/article/fbi-chris-wray-testify-capitol-riot -9a5539af34b15338bb5c4923907eeb67

Van Gordon Martin (2011, January 25). *No limit to love* [Album]. Van Gordon Martin.

Warren, R. (2006). *The Purpose Driven Life* (p. 265). Findaway World.

Wegeler, F. (1987). *Beethoven remembered: The biographical notes of Franz Wegeler and Ferdinand Ries* (p.94), trans. F. Noonan. Great Ocean Publishers.

West Point United States Military Academy (2023, n.d.). *West Point cadet honor code and honor system.* West Point United States Military Academy. https://www.westpoint.edu/military /simon-center-for-the-professional-military-ethic/honor

Wilton, D. (2020, December 30). *Hero.* Wordorigins.org. https:// www.wordorigins.org/big-list-entries/hero. Note: The English word "hero" is gender neutral.

Wohlleben, P. (2016). *The hidden life of trees: What they feel, how they communicate—Discoveries from a secret world* (Vol. 1, p. 17). Greystone Books.

Yang, J. & Kahn, S (2022, April 26). How powerful conservatives pushed the "Big Lie" that the 2020 election was fraudulent. PBS News Hour. https://www.pbs.org/newshour/show/how-powerful-conservatives-pushed-the-big-lie-that-the-2020-election-was-fraudulent

Index

Gratitude

My heart is filled with gratitude for the love and support of so many people from all aspects and times of my life. The names and stories of all would fill many books. Please know I deeply appreciate every person and the contributions each of you has made to my life.

To Vivian Perry Gordon (my mom) and Oscar Roland Gordon (my dad), my deepest love for your sacrifices for me to have the educational experiences not afforded to either of you.

To the students of William G. Enloe High School 1968—1970, thank you for selecting me to serve in student government. This first leadership opportunity changed my life's journey in profoundly positive ways.

To my teachers and mentors especially Ms. Lucy Cone, Ms. Edith Lee Tippet, Ms. Carlie Brown, Mr. Delma Blinson, Dr. Paul Brandes, Dr. Pat Jarrard, Professor Martha Nell Hardy, Dr. June Gallessich, and Dr. Warren Bennis; thank you for seeing my potential and helping me grow.

To Clients

Thank you to each client I have been blessed to partner with to improve individual leadership, team and organizational effectiveness. Trusting me as your coach and organizational development consultant is the greatest gift of my career.

To Leaders Interviewed for Being the Real Deal

For over 20 years, leaders have graciously shared their time and wisdom with me as I worked on articulating what it takes to be the real deal as a leader in a challenging and rapidly changing global leadership landscape—thank you! A special note of appreciation to each of the following leaders* for your time and insights:

Brenda C. Barnes, Chairman and CEO, Sara Lee Corporation; Gregory Q. Brown, President and Co-CEO, Motorola; Susan Crown, Chairman and Founder, SCE; Craig J. Duchossis, Chairman, Director, and CEO, The Duchossis Group; Jeff M. Fettig, Chairman and CEO, Whirlpool Corporation; William D. Green, Chairman and CEO, Accenture; E. Neville Isdell, Chairman, The Board of Directors, Coca-Cola Company; Jerry Jurgensen, CEO, Nationwide; Gary C. Kelly, Chairman, President, and CEO, Southwest Airlines; Robert W. Lane, Chairman and CEO, Deere & Company; Andrew N. Liveris, Chairman and CEO, The Dow Chemical Company; Githesh Ramamurthy, CEO and Chairman, CCC Intelligent Solutions; John W. Rowe, Chairman and CEO Exelon Corporation; Ivan G. Seidenberg Chairman and CEO, Verizon Communications; Mayo A. Shattuck III, Chairman, President, and CEO, Constellation Energy; James D. Sinegal, Cofounder, President, Director and CEO, Costco Wholesale Corporation; Jim A. Skinner, Vice Chairman, and CEO, McDonald's Corporation; Frederick W. Smith, Chairman, President, and CEO, FedEx; David B. Speer, Chairman and CEO, Illinois Tool Works; Frederick H. Waddell President, Director, and CEO, Northern Trust Corporation; Thomas J. Wilson, Chair, President, and CEO, Allstate; Patricia A. Woertz, Chairman, President, and CEO, Archer Daniels Midland Company; Stephen P. Zelnak, Jr., Chairman and CEO, Martin Marietta Materials.

*Leaders are listed alphabetically with titles listed at the time of interviews for this book.

To the "Get It Done" Team

Coach Penny Wand, team captain—your coaching wisdom and honest feedback gently held my feet to the fire to finish this book.

Fellow Chainsaw Chick Morgan Gleason and soon-to-be Ph.D.—your superpowers on endnotes, bibliography, and manuscript with artwork notated accomplished tasks I could not do.

Creative Missi Jay, Giggle Box Designs—your artistic talents brought the oak tree metaphor to life throughout the book making the artwork an inspiring part of *Being the Real Deal*.

Design Guru Ipek Erodogan-Trinkaus—your design expertise and creative insights were essential to making the final version reflect the book's messages.

For all the Amazing work and loving friendship—*Coach Penny, Chainsaw Chick Morgan, Creative Missi, and Design Guru Ipek*—with your work, encouragement and laughter—we "got it done."

You are all "Simply the Best"!

To My Gordon Group Teammates

We accomplished the highest quality work for our clients with passion, laughter, crazy hats and attitude pins, more than a few late nights doing "just one more revision," and champagne celebrations. I am thankful for each of your contributions to achieving major transformations for our clients even when the challenges seemed impossible at the beginning.

To Dr. Barbara Martin Fossum and Ms. Trisha Svehla an extra special shout-out of appreciation for all the support, leadership, expertise, and willingness to dare to take on big challenges with me. Best not to put in print all the many times and reasons both of you have saved me—just know I am forever grateful.

To each of the following teammates, know you made a difference for our clients and me: John (Jay) Feld, Ron Hart, Cathy O'Sullivan, Lori Lichtman-Sander, Julie Allgood-Youngs, Terri L. Cramer, Tracy L. Hurst, Jessica Joslin, Chrissy Hodges-Chakrani, Michael Mandziuk, Catalina Rivera, Tosh Marie Bonete, Kristian (Sam) Benig, Stefania Gelazius, Emilie Baliozian, Steve Rish, Yoko Takamoto, and Alex Piegza.

To the 5 W Club

President Charles C. Crutchfield, and official guardian angel; thank you for the introduction to *The Artist Way*, morning pages, books on writing, trips through the rabbit hole, adventuring, hanging on cliffs with the wind beneath our wings and so much more!

Sargent-at-Arms Dr. Susan Boseman Roberts—thank you, my sister (by another mother) for your love and support as we have traveled life's roads from our Tarheel roots to our northern exposures. Yes, I appreciate all your sage advice especially "hindsight is always 50/50."

To My Family

Dr. Don Martin, husband, and best friend for more than 43 years; thank you for your love and support from our Texas start to today enabling "together anything is possible" to be true. From your encouragement to start writing with a gift of a simple notebook for stories to cheerleading to keep writing, to notebooks with trees on the cover, study halls in the cold Chicago winters, reading draft after draft, and never giving up on me finishing my book has made all the difference. For starting each morning with a new, blank sheet of paper beginning anew our life's journey together, know I love you.

Van Gordon Martin, our son; thank you for being the Vice President of Fun for the Gordon Group and for your inspiring music which lights the way forward for all of us to a better world. *Calling Out* for love, justice, unity and equality for all is what you sing. Yes, *Take the High Road* though not easy is what living a life of integrity requires of all of us. *Let It Grow* calls for the root of humanity to be love and to let love grow. As your first album title proclaims—there is *No Limit to Love* (www.vangordonmartin.com). No words can adequately express my unconditional love for you. Van—you are my inspiration!

About the Author

As a pioneer in leadership coaching, Dr. Vicky Gordon has spent the last 40 years helping thousands of individuals build their leadership capabilities. In this book, Vicky weaves together her real-life leadership coaching stories, leadership research, and personal leadership journey from the tobacco fields of North Carolina to the ivory towers of academia to office cubicles  and boardrooms to founding her firm. Her practical coaching paints a portrait of inspiring leadership.

Dr. Vicky Gordon, Ph. D., is the Founder and CEO of her Chicago-based leadership coaching and organizational development firm. As a pioneering female entrepreneur and leadership coach, Vicky's clients range from Fortune 500 CEOs to front-line leaders. From high tech to healthcare, from the shop floor to the C-Suite, hundreds of organizations and thousands of individuals have called "Dr. Vicky" their partner in achieving transformational change.

DrVickyGordon.com
linkedin.com/in/drvickygordon
instagram.com/drvickygordon